Glencoe Science

California
4-in-1 Lab Manual

CALIFORNIA GRADE 8

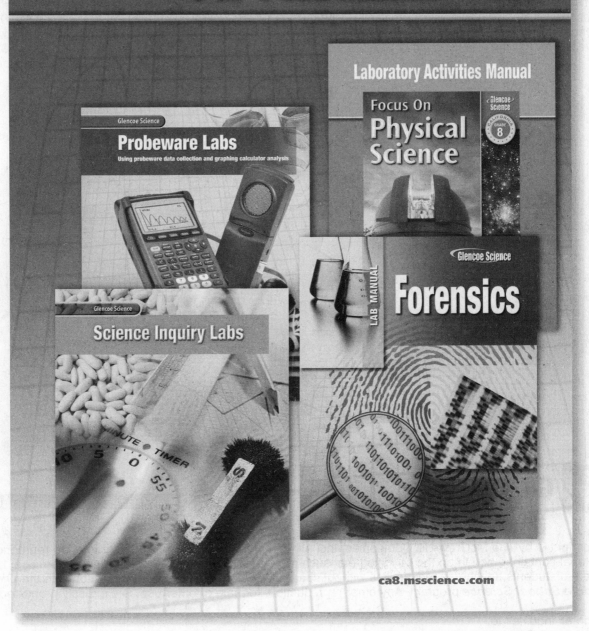

Laboratory Activities Manual

Glencoe Science
Probeware Labs
Using probeware data collection and graphing calculator analysis

Focus On
Physical Science
Glencoe Science CALIFORNIA GRADE 8

Glencoe Science
Science Inquiry Labs

Glencoe Science
LAB MANUAL
Forensics

ca8.msscience.com

Mc Graw Hill **Glencoe**

New York, New York   Columbus, Ohio   Chicago, Illinois

Glencoe Science

Credits

The photo of the CBL 2, graphing calculator, and pH probe on the front cover and at the top of the first page of each student lab appears courtesy of Texas Instruments, Inc. Each Probeware Activity was reviewed by Richard Sorensen of Vernier Software & Technology.

The terms CBL 2, TI-GRAPH LINK, TI Connect and TI InterActive! are either registered trademarks of, trademarks of, or copyrighted by Texas Instruments, Inc. Vernier LabPro is a registered trademark of Graphical Analysis and EasyData copyrighted by Vernier Software & Technology. Macintosh is a registered trademark of Apple Computer, Inc. Windows is a registered trademark of Microsoft Corporation in the United States and/or other countries.

 Glencoe

The McGraw-Hill Companies

Send all inquiries to:
Glencoe/McGraw-Hill
8787 Orion Place
Columbus, OH 43240

ISBN-13: 978-0-07-879442-1
ISBN-10: 0-07-879442-0

Printed in the United States of America.

7 RHR 13 12

Table of Contents

LABORATORY ACTIVITIES

INQUIRY ACTIVITIES

FORENSICS ACTIVITIES

PROBEWARE ACTIVITIES

To the Student

Glencoe's 4-in-1 Lab Manual provides you with four separate sections of labs. While each section is unique, all the lab activities in this manual require your active participation. You will test hypotheses, collect and apply data, and discover new information. You will use many different skills to make connections between the lab activities and what you already know.

The *Laboratory Activities* will help you focus your efforts on gathering information, obtaining data from the environment, and making observations. You will also work on organizing your data so conclusions can be drawn in a way that is easily repeated by other scientists.

The *Inquiry Activities* will help you understand that no science works alone. A scientist cannot explain how a plant makes food just by knowing the parts of the leaf. Someone needs to know how the chemicals in the leaf work. Knowledge of Earth science, life science, and physical science is needed for a full explanation of how the leaf makes food. Today, teams of scientists solve problems. Each scientist uses his or her knowledge of Earth science, life science, or physical science to find solutions to problems in areas such as the environment or health.

The *Forensics Activities* provide in-depth investigations that deal with DNA, collecting and analyzing data, and interpreting evidence found at a crime or accident scene. You will use your knowledge of scientific inquiry and your problem-solving skills as you learn about forensics procedures. You will then apply these procedures to real-world scenarios.

The *Probeware Activities* are designed to help you study science using probeware technology. A probeware lab is different from other labs because it uses a probe or sensor to collect data, a data collection unit to interpret and store the data, and a graphing calculator or computer to analyze the data. These components are connected with a software program called DataMate that makes them work together in an easy-to-use, handheld system. These labs are designed specifically for the TI-73 or TI-83 Plus graphing calculators and a CBL 2™ (produced by Texas Instruments, Inc.) or LabPro® (produced by Vernier Software & Technology) data collection unit.

Getting Started

Science is the body of information including all the hypotheses and experiments that tell us about our environment. All people involved in scientific work use similar methods for gaining information. One important scientific skill is the ability to obtain data directly from the environment. Observations must be based on what occurs in the environment. Equally important is the ability to organize these data into a form from which valid conclusions can be drawn. These conclusions must be such that other scientists can achieve the same results in the laboratory.

To make the most of your laboratory experience, you need to continually work to increase your laboratory skills. These skills include the ability to recognize and use equipment properly and to measure and use SI units accurately. Safety must also be an ongoing concern. To help you get started in discovering many fascinating things about the world around you, the next few pages provide you with the following:

- a visual overview of basic **laboratory equipment** for you to label
- a reference sheet of **safety symbols**
- a list of your **safety responsibilities** in the laboratory
- a **safety contract**
- a reference sheet of **SI units**

Each lab activity in this manual includes the following sections:

- an investigation **title** and introductory section providing information about the problem under study
- a **strategy** section identifying the **objective(s)** of the activity
- a list of needed **materials**
- safety concerns identified with **safety icons** and **caution statements**
- a set of step-by-step **procedures**
- a section to help you record your **data and observations**
- a section to help you **analyze your data** and record your **conclusions**
- a closing **strategy check** so that you can review your achievement of the objectives of the activity

Laboratory Equipment

Figure 1

1. _____   2. _____

3. _____

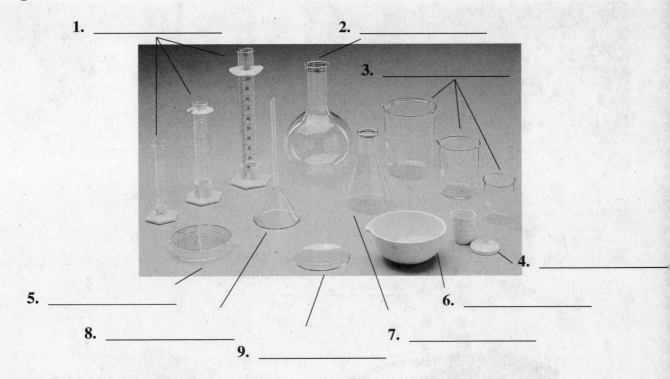

5. _____

8. _____   9. _____   7. _____   6. _____

4. _____

Figure 2

1. _____

3. _____   2. _____

4. _____

5. _____   6. _____

7. _____

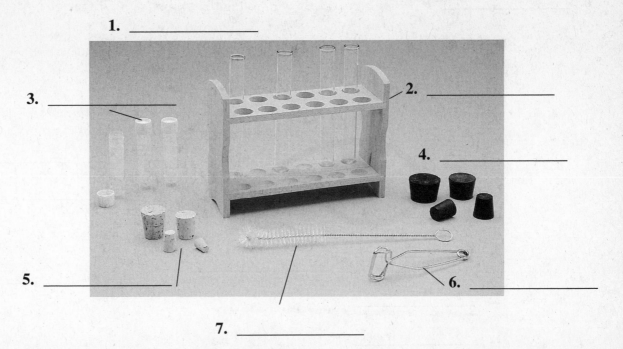

Laboratory Equipment (continued)

Figure 3

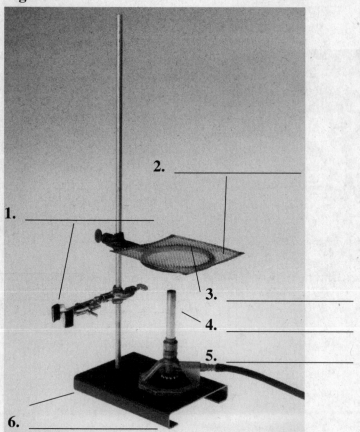

1. _____
2. _____
3. _____
4. _____
5. _____
6. _____

Figure 4

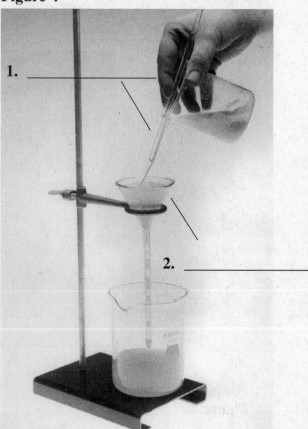

1. _____
2. _____

Figure 5

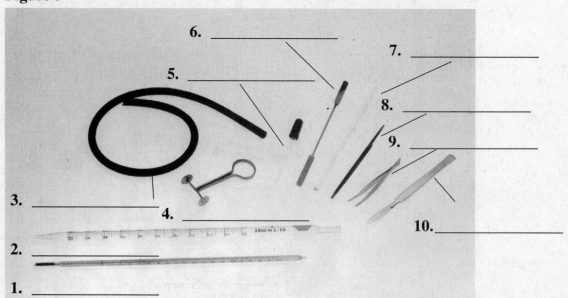

1. _____
2. _____
3. _____
4. _____
5. _____
6. _____
7. _____
8. _____
9. _____
10. _____

Laboratory Equipment (continued)

Figure 6

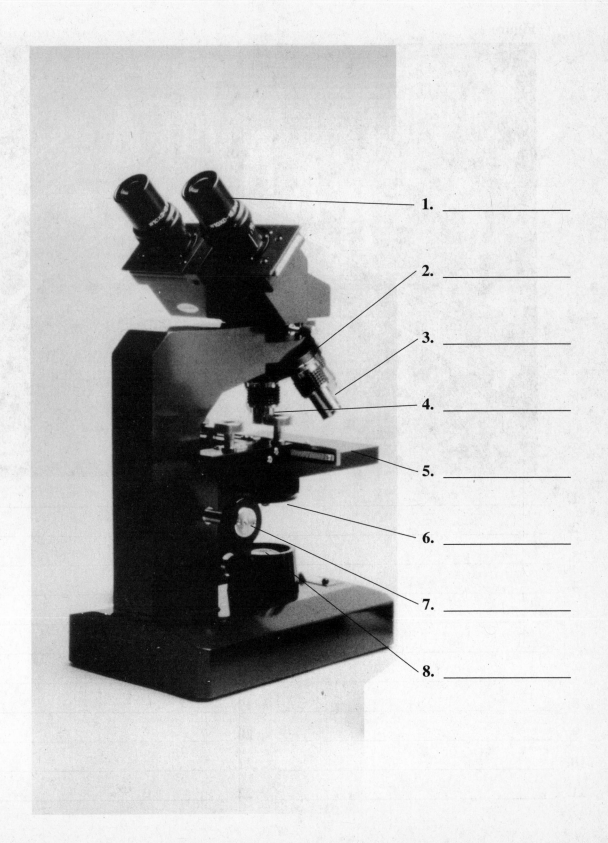

1. _____

2. _____

3. _____

4. _____

5. _____

6. _____

7. _____

8. _____

Laboratory Equipment (continued)

Figure 7

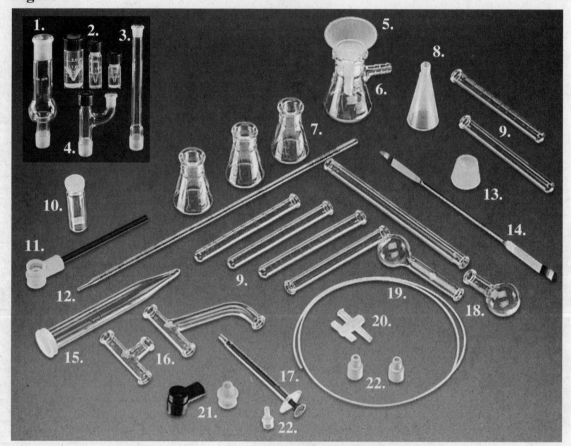

1. _____
2. _____
3. _____
4. _____
5. _____
6. _____
7. _____
8. _____
9. _____
10. _____
11. _____

12. _____
13. _____
14. _____
15. _____
16. _____
17. _____
18. _____
19. _____
20. _____
21. _____
22. _____

Laboratory Equipment (continued)

Figure 8

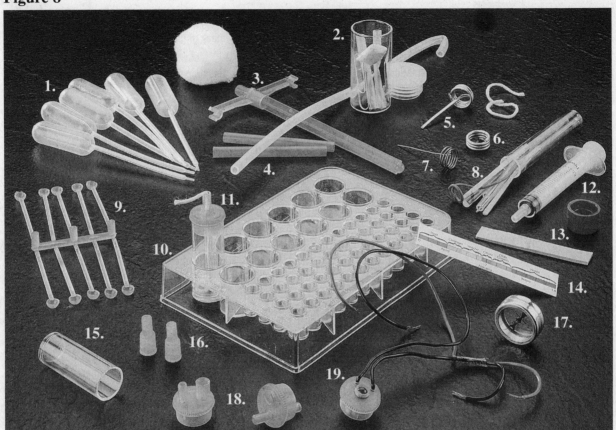

1. _____
2. _____
3. _____
4. _____
5. _____
6. _____
7. _____
8. _____
9. _____
10. _____

11. _____
12. _____
13. _____
14. _____
15. _____
16. _____
17. _____
18. _____
19. _____

SAFETY SYMBOLS

SAFETY SYMBOLS	HAZARD	EXAMPLES	PRECAUTION	REMEDY
DISPOSAL	Special disposal procedures need to be followed.	certain chemicals, living organisms	Do not dispose of these materials in the sink or trash can.	Dispose of wastes as directed by your teacher.
BIOLOGICAL	Organisms or other biological materials that might be harmful to humans	bacteria, fungi, blood, unpreserved tissues, plant materials	Avoid skin contact with these materials. Wear mask or gloves.	Notify your teacher if you suspect contact with material. Wash hands thoroughly.
EXTREME TEMPERATURE	Objects that can burn skin by being too cold or too hot	boiling liquids, hot plates, dry ice, liquid nitrogen	Use proper protection when handling.	Go to your teacher for first aid.
SHARP OBJECT	Use of tools or glassware that can easily puncture or slice skin	razor blades, pins, scalpels, pointed tools, dissecting probes, broken glass	Practice common-sense behavior and follow guidelines for use of the tool.	Go to your teacher for first aid.
FUME	Possible danger to respiratory tract from fumes	ammonia, acetone, nail polish remover, heated sulfur, moth balls	Make sure there is good ventilation. Never smell fumes directly. Wear a mask.	Leave foul area and notify your teacher immediately.
ELECTRICAL	Possible danger from electrical shock or burn	improper grounding, liquid spills, short circuits, exposed wires	Double-check setup with teacher. Check condition of wires and apparatus.	Do not attempt to fix electrical problems. Notify your teacher immediately.
IRRITANT	Substances that can irritate the skin or mucous membranes of the respiratory tract	pollen, moth balls, steel wool, fiberglass, potassium permanganate	Wear dust mask and gloves. Practice extra care when handling these materials.	Go to your teacher for first aid.
CHEMICAL	Chemicals can react with and destroy tissue and other materials	bleaches such as hydrogen peroxide; acids such as sulfuric acid, hydrochloric acid; bases such as ammonia, sodium hydroxide	Wear goggles, gloves, and an apron.	Immediately flush the affected area with water and notify your teacher.
TOXIC	Substance may be poisonous if touched, inhaled, or swallowed.	mercury, many metal compounds, iodine, poinsettia plant parts	Follow your teacher's instructions.	Always wash hands thoroughly after use. Go to your teacher for first aid.
FLAMMABLE	Flammable chemicals may be ignited by open flame, spark, or exposed heat.	alcohol, kerosene, potassium permanganate	Avoid open flames and heat when using flammable chemicals.	Notify your teacher immediately. Use fire safety equipment if applicable.
OPEN FLAME	Open flame in use, may cause fire.	hair, clothing, paper, synthetic materials	Tie back hair and loose clothing. Follow teacher's instruction on lighting and extinguishing flames.	Notify your teacher immediately. Use fire safety equipment if applicable.

Eye Safety
Proper eye protection should be worn at all times by anyone performing or observing science activities.

Clothing Protection
This symbol appears when substances could stain or burn clothing.

Animal Safety
This symbol appears when safety of animals and students must be ensured.

Handwashing
After the lab, wash hands with soap and water before removing goggles.

Student Laboratory and Safety Guidelines

Regarding Emergencies

- Inform the teacher immediately of *any* mishap—fire, injury, glassware breakage, chemical spills, etc.
- Follow your teacher's instructions and your school's procedures in dealing with emergencies.

Regarding Your Person

- Do NOT wear clothing that is loose enough to catch on anything, and avoid sandals or open-toed shoes.
- Wear protective safety gloves, goggles, and aprons as instructed.
- Always wear safety goggles (not glasses) when using hazardous chemicals.
- Wear goggles throughout the entire activity, cleanup, and handwashing.
- Keep your hands away from your face while working in the laboratory.
- Remove synthetic fingernails before working in the lab (these are highly flammable).
- Do NOT use hair spray, mousse, or other flammable hair products just before or during laboratory work where an open flame is used (they can ignite easily).
- Tie back long hair and loose clothing to keep them away from flames and equipment.
- Remove loose jewelry—chains or bracelets—while doing lab work.
- NEVER eat or drink while in the lab or store food in lab equipment or the lab refrigerator.
- Do NOT inhale vapors or taste, touch, or smell any chemical or substance unless instructed to do so by your teacher.

Regarding Your Work

- Read all instructions before you begin a laboratory or field activity. Ask questions if you do not understand any part of the activity.
- Work ONLY on activities assigned by your teacher.
- Do NOT substitute other chemicals/substances for those listed in your activity.
- Do NOT begin any activity until directed to do so by your teacher.
- Do NOT handle any equipment without specific permission.
- Remain in your own work area unless given permission by your teacher to leave it.
- Do NOT point heated containers—test tubes, flasks, etc.—at yourself or anyone else.
- Do NOT take any materials or chemicals out of the classroom.
- Stay out of storage areas unless you are instructed to be there and are supervised by your teacher.
- NEVER work alone in the laboratory.
- When using dissection equipment, always cut away from yourself and others. Cut downward, never stabbing at the object.
- Handle living organisms or preserved specimens only when authorized by your teacher.
- Always wear heavy gloves when handling animals. If you are bitten or stung, notify your teacher immediately.

Regarding Cleanup

- Keep work and lab areas clean, limiting the amount of easily ignitable materials.
- Turn off all burners and other equipment before leaving the lab.
- Carefully dispose of waste materials as instructed by your teacher.
- Wash your hands thoroughly with soap and warm water after each activity.

Student Science Laboratory Safety Contract

I agree to:

- Act responsibly at all times in the laboratory.
- Follow all instructions given, orally or in writing, by my teacher.
- Perform only those activities assigned and approved by my teacher.
- Protect my eyes, face, hands, and body by wearing proper clothing and using protective equipment provided by my school.
- Carry out good housekeeping practices as instructed by my teacher.
- Know the location of safety and first-aid equipment in the laboratory.
- Notify my teacher immediately of an emergency.
- NEVER work alone in the laboratory.
- NEVER eat or drink in the laboratory unless instructed to do so by my teacher.
- Handle living organisms or preserved specimens only when authorized by my teacher, and then, with respect.
- NEVER enter or work in a supply area unless instructed to do so and supervised by my teacher.

[This portion of the contract is to be kept by the student.]

[Return this portion to your teacher.]

I, _____, [print name] have read each of the statements in the Student Science Laboratory Safety Contract and understand these safety rules. I agree to abide by the safety regulations and any additional written or verbal instructions provided by the school district or my teacher. I further agree to follow all other written and verbal instructions given in class.

_____   _____

              Student Signature   Date

I acknowledge that my child/ward has signed this contract in good faith.

_____   _____

         Parent/Guardian Signature   Date

SI Reference Sheet

The International System of Units (SI) is accepted as the standard for measurement throughout most of the world. Sometimes quantities are measured using different SI units. In order to use them together in an equation, you must convert all of the quantities into the same unit. To convert, you multiply by a conversion factor. A conversion factor is a ratio that is equal to one. Make a conversion factor by building a ratio of equivalent units. Place the new units in the numerator and the old units in the denominator. For example, to convert 1.255 L to mL, multiply 1.255 L by the appropriate ratio as follows:

$$1.255 \text{ L} \times 1{,}000 \text{ mL}/1 \text{ L} = 1{,}255 \text{ mL}$$

In this equation, the unit L cancels just as if it were a number.

Frequently used SI units are listed in **Table 1.**

Table 1

Frequently Used SI Units	
Length	1 millimeter (mm) = 100 micrometers (μm) 1 centimeter (cm) = 10 millimeters (mm) 1 meter (m) = 100 centimeters (cm) 1 kilometer (km) = 1,000 meters (m) 1 light-year = 9,460,000,000,000 kilometers (km)
Area	1 square meter (m^2) = 10,000 square centimeters (cm^2) 1 square kilometer (km^2) = 1,000,000 square meters (m^2)
Volume	1 milliliter (mL) = 1 cubic centimeter (cm^3) 1 liter (L) = 1,000 milliliters (mL)
Mass	1 gram (g) = 1,000 milligrams (mg) 1 kilogram (kg) = 1,000 grams (g) 1 metric ton = 1,000 kilograms (kg)
Time	1 s = 1 second

Several other supplementary SI units are listed in **Table 2.**

Table 2

Supplementary SI Units			
Measurement	**Unit**	**Symbol**	**Expressed in base units**
Energy	joule	J	$kg \cdot m^2/s^2$
Force	newton	N	$kg \cdot m/s^2$
Power	watt	W	$kg \cdot m^2/s^3$ or J/s
Pressure	pascal	Pa	$kg/m \cdot s^2$ or $N \cdot m$

Temperature measurements in SI often are made in degrees Celsius. Celsius temperature is a supplementary unit derived from the base unit kelvin. The Celsius scale (°C) has 100 equal graduations between the freezing temperature (0°C) and the boiling temperature of water (100°C). The following relationship exists between the Celsius and kelvin temperature scales:

$$K = °C + 273$$

Figure 1

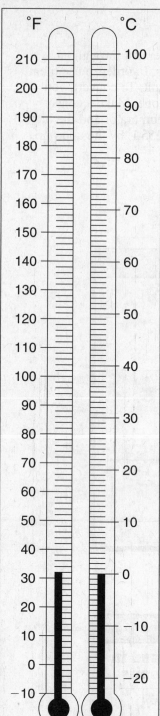

To convert from °F to °C, you can:

1. For exact amounts, use the equation at the bottom of **Table 3**

OR

2. For approximate amounts, find °F on the thermometer at the left of **Figure 1** and determine °C on the thermometer at the right.

Table 3

SI Metric to English Conversions			
	When you want to convert:	**Multiply by:**	**To find:**
Length	inches	2.54	centimeters
	centimeters	0.39	inches
	feet	0.30	meters
	meters	3.28	feet
	yards	0.91	meters
	meters	1.09	yards
	miles	1.61	kilometers
	kilometers	0.62	miles
Mass and weight*	ounces	28.35	grams
	grams	0.04	ounces
	pounds	0.45	kilograms
	kilograms	2.20	pounds
	tons	0.91	metric tons
	metric tons	1.10	tons
	pounds	4.45	newtons
	newtons	0.23	pounds
Volume	cubic inches	16.39	cubic centimeters
	milliliters	0.06	cubic inches
	cubic feet	0.03	cubic meters
	cubic meters	35.31	cubic feet
	liters	1.06	quarts
	liters	0.26	gallons
	gallons	3.78	liters
Area	square inches	6.45	square centimeters
	square centimeters	0.16	square inches
	square feet	0.09	square meters
	square meters	10.76	square feet
	square miles	2.59	square kilometers
	square kilometers	0.39	square miles
	hectares	2.47	acres
	acres	0.40	hectares
Temperature	Fahrenheit	$\frac{5}{9}(°F - 32)$	Celsius
	Celsius	$\frac{9}{5}°C + 32$	Fahrenheit

* Weight as measured in standard Earth gravity

Laboratory Activities

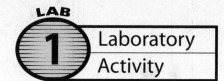

Pushing People Around

When we push something, we unconsciously compensate for how much mass it has. We know that if an object has a larger mass it will require more force to get it moving and if it has a small mass it will require less force. But how much difference is there? In this experiment, we will see what variables affect acceleration.

Strategy

You will see what happens when you use a constant force to pull a skater.
You will examine the relationship between force, acceleration, and mass.

Materials

tape
meter stick
roller skates
skating safety equipment (helmet, pads)
spring balance
stopwatch

Procedure

1. Mark positions on the floor at intervals of 0 m, 5 m, 10 m, and 15 m with the tape. The floor should be smooth, straight, and level.

2. Have one student stand on the 0-m mark with the skates on. A second student stands behind the mark and holds the skater. The skater holds the spring balance by its hook.

3. The third student holds the other end of the spring balance and exerts a constant pulling force on the skater. When the skater is released, the puller must maintain a constant force throughout the distance. Measure the time to each of the marks. Record this in the Data and Observations section along with the spring balance readings at each mark.

4. Repeat steps 2 and 3 for two different skaters in order to vary the mass. Keep the force the same. Make sure the skaters hold their skates parallel and do not try to change direction during the trial.

5. Repeat steps 2, 3, and 4 with a different constant force. Use the same three skaters. Record these results in the Data and Observations section.

Copyright © Glencoe/McGraw-Hill, a division of The McGraw-Hill Companies, Inc.

SCI 1.c. Students know how to solve problems involving distance, time, and average speed.
Also covers **SCI 1.a.**

Laboratory Activity 1 (continued)

Data and Observations

Table 1

Trial	Distance (m)	Force (N)	Time (s)
		Roller Skater Distance, Trial 1	
	5		
1	10		
	15		
	5		
2	10		
	15		
	5		
3	10		
	15		

Table 2

Trial	Distance (m)	Force (N)	Time (s)
		Roller Skater Distance, Trial 2	
	5		
1	10		
	15		
	5		
2	10		
	15		
	5		
3	10		
	15		

Laboratory Activity 1 (continued)

Questions and Conclusions

1. Until the time of Galileo and Newton, people believed that, disregarding friction, a constant force was required to produce a constant speed. Do your observations confirm or reject this notion?

_____

_____

2. What happens to the speed as you proceed farther along the measured distance?

_____

3. What happens to the rate of increase in speed—the acceleration—as you proceed farther along the measured distance?

_____

4. When the force is the same, how does the acceleration depend upon the mass?

_____

5. When the mass of the skater is the same, how does the acceleration depend upon the force?

_____

6. Suppose a 4-N force is applied to the skater and no movement results. How can this be explained?

_____

_____

Strategy Check

_____ Can you pull someone with a constant force?

_____ Can you explain the relationship between force, mass, and acceleration?

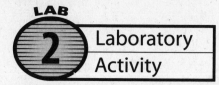

Motion of a Bowling Ball

LAB 2 Laboratory Activity

It takes time to walk somewhere. Sometimes you move quickly, while other times you move slowly. Other objects might show variation in their movement as well. In this lab, you will graph the movement of a bowling ball and consider how its motion relates to other kinds of motion.

Strategy

You will make a distance versus time graph of a bowling ball as it rolls.
You will relate the motion of the bowling ball to other types of motion.

Materials

bowling ball
stopwatches (5–10)
large pillow

Procedure

1. Line up with other students at equally spaced distances of 1m. Your teacher will mark the distances.
2. At the far end of the hall, set up the pillow or other large, soft object. This will prevent the ball from rolling too far.
3. Start your stopwatch when your teacher rolls the ball slowly.
4. When the ball passes you, stop your stopwatch. As the ball passes the other students, they will do the same.

5. Record all of your times in Table 1.
6. Clear your stopwatch to prepare for another trial. This time, your teacher will roll the ball faster.
7. Record your times in Table 2.
8. Graph the data for both tables, putting the data from Table 1 into Graph 1, and the data from Table 2 into Graph 2. Place the distance on the vertical axis, and the time on the horizontal axis.

Data and Observations

Trial 1	
Distance	**Time**
0 m	
1 m	
2 m	
3 m	
4 m	
5 m	

Trial 2	
Distance	**Time**
0 m	
1 m	
2 m	
3 m	
4 m	
5 m	

 SCI 1.f. Students know how to interpret graphs of position versus time and graphs of speed versus time for motion in a single direction. Also covers **SCI 1.c.**

Laboratory Activity 2 (continued)

Graph 1

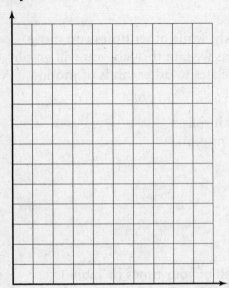

Graph 2

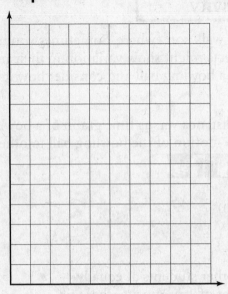

Questions and Conclusions

1. What do you notice about the graphs of the two trials?

_____

_____

2. On a distance versus time graph, what does the slope of the line tell you?

_____

_____

3. On a distance versus time graph, what does a flat (horizontal) line mean?

_____

4. Imagine a bowling ball dropped from a great height. How would the motion of this bowling ball relate to the bowling balls in the lab?

_____

_____

_____

5. What was the speed of the bowling ball in the first trial? In the second trial?

_____

_____

Laboratory Activity 2 (continued)

6. What distance did the bowling balls travel? What is their displacement?

_____

_____

7. How are distance and displacement related?

_____

_____

Strategy Check

_____ Can you graph the speed of an object in motion?

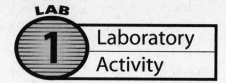

LAB 1
Laboratory Activity

Projectile Motion

What do a volleyball, baseball, tennis ball, soccer ball, and football have in common? Each is used in a sport and each is a projectile after it is tapped, thrown, kicked, or hit. A projectile is any object that is thrown or shot into the air. If air resistance is ignored, the only force acting on a projectile is the force of gravity.

The path followed by a projectile is called a trajectory. Figure 1a shows the shape of the trajectory of a toy rocket. Because the force of gravity is the only force acting on it, the toy rocket has an acceleration of 9.80 m/s² downward. However, the motion of the projectile is upward and then downward. Figure 1b shows the size and direction of the vertical velocity of a toy rocket at different moments along its trajectory. The rocket's velocity upward begins to decrease immediately after launch and the rocket begins to slow down. The rocket continues to slow down. And then, for an instant at the highest point of its trajectory, it stops moving because its velocity upward is zero. As the rocket begins to fall, its velocity begins to increase downward.

As you can see, the shape of the upward trajectory of the rocket is a mirror-image of the shape of its downward trajectory. Can the trajectory of a toy rocket be used to learn something about the motion of a projectile? In this experiment you will find out.

Strategy

You will measure the flight times of a projectile.
You will analyze the flight times of a projectile.

Materials

toy water rocket and launcher
bucket of water
3 stopwatches

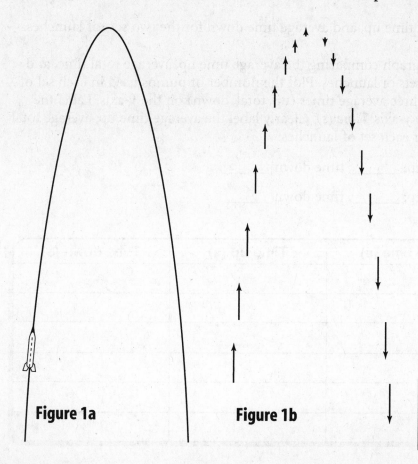

Figure 1a   **Figure 1b**

> **SCI 2.e.** Students know that when the forces on an object are unbalanced, the object will change its velocity (that is, it will speed up, slow down, or change direction). Also covers **SCI 2.f.**

Laboratory Activity 1 (continued)

Procedure

1. Wear goggles during this experiment.
2. Fill the water rocket to the level line shown on the rocket's body. Always fill the rocket to the same level during each flight in the experiment.
3. Attach the pump/launcher to the rocket as shown in the manufacturer's directions.
4. Pump the pump/launcher 10 times. **CAUTION:** *Do not exceed 20 pumps or the maximum number suggested by the manufacturer, whichever is lower. Be sure to hold the rocket and pump/launcher so that the rocket is not directed toward yourself or another person.*
5. Launch the rocket vertically. Predict the time for the rocket to rise to its highest point, and the time for it to fall back to Earth. Now predict these times if the rocket is pumped 15 times. Record your predictions as time up and time down in the Data and Observations section.

6. Retrieve the rocket. Fill the rocket with water as in step 2. Pump the pump/launcher 10 times. Record the number of pumps in Table 1.
7. At a given signal to the timers, launch the rocket. Your teacher will have timers measure specific parts of the flight using stopwatches. Record the values measured by the timers as total time, time up, and time down in Table 1.
8. Repeat steps 6 and 7 twice.
9. Repeat steps 6 and 7 three more times, increasing the number of pumps to 15 for each launch. **CAUTION:** *Do not exceed the maximum number of pumps suggested by the manufacturer.*

Data and Observations

1. Calculate the average total time, time up, and average time down for the two sets of launches. Record these values in Table 2.
2. Use Graph 1 to construct a bar graph comparing the average time up, average total time, and average time down for the two sets of launches. Plot the number of pumps used in each set of launches on the *x*-axis and the three average times (up, total, down) on the *y*-axis. Label the *x*-axis *Number of pumps* and the *y*-axis *Time (s)*. Clearly label the average time up, average total time, and average time down for each set of launches.

10 pumps—Prediction of time up: _____; time down _____

15 pumps—Prediction of time up: _____; time down _____

Table 1

Number of pumps	Total time (s)	Time up (s)	Time down (s)

Laboratory Activity 1 (continued)

Table 2

Number of pumps	Average total time (s)	Average time up (s)	Average time down (s)

Graph 1

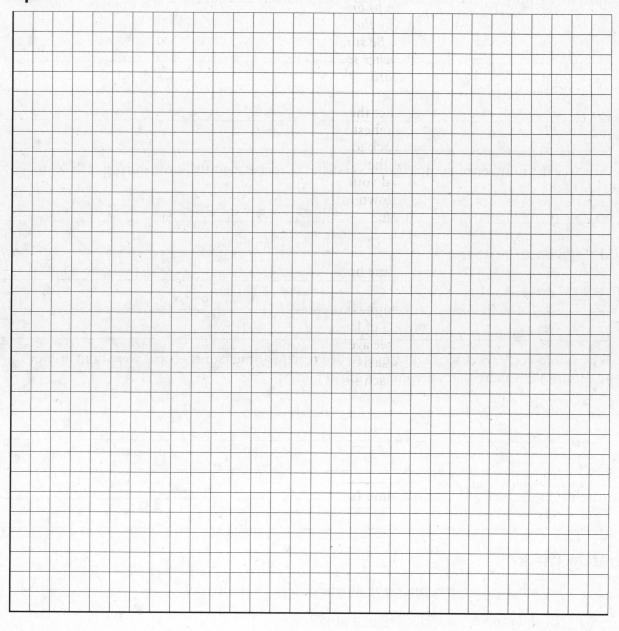

Laboratory Activity 1 (continued)

Questions and Conclusions

1. How well did your predictions agree with the measured times?

_____

_____

_____

2. Do your graphs support the statement that the time for a projectile to reach its highest point is equal to the time for the projectile to fall back to Earth? Explain.

_____

_____

_____

_____

3. Why was the number of pumps used to launch the rocket kept the same during each set of launches?

_____

_____

_____

_____

4. Why would you expect the flight times to be greater for the launches that were done using 15 pumps than those that were done with 10 pumps?

_____

_____

_____

_____

Strategy Check

_____ Can you measure and analyze the flight times of a projectile?

_____ Can you predict the trajectory of a projectile?

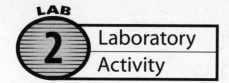

Velocity and Momentum

LAB 2 Laboratory Activity

As you know, you can increase the speed of a shopping cart by pushing harder on its handles. You can also increase its speed by pushing on the handles for a longer time. Both ways will increase the momentum of the cart. How is the momentum of an object related to the time that a force acts on it? In this experiment, you will investigate that question.

Strategy

You will observe the effect of a net force on a cart.
You will measure the velocity of the cart at various times.
You will determine the momentum of the cart.
You will relate the momentum of the cart and the time during which the force acted on it.

Materials

utility clamp
ring stand
2 plastic-coated wire ties (1 short, 1 long)
pulley
metric balance
momentum cart
2–3 rubber bands
1-m length of string

100-g mass
3–4 books
plastic foam sheet
meterstick
masking tape
stopwatch/timer
felt-tip marker

Procedure

1. Attach the utility clamp to the ring stand. Using the short plastic-coated wire tie, attach the pulley to the clamp.
2. Use the metric balance to find the mass of the cart. Record this value in the Data and Observations section on the line provided.
3. Wrap the rubber bands around the cart lengthwise.
4. Tie one end of the string around the rubber bands as shown in Figure 1. Tie a loop at the opposite end of the string. Pass the string over the pulley.

5. Wrap the long plastic-coated wire tie securely around the 100-g mass. Attach the mass to the loop on the string with the wire tie.
6. Place the ring stand near the edge of the table. Adjust the position of the pulley so that the string is parallel to the table top as shown in Figure 2. Be sure that the 100-g mass can fall freely to the floor. Place several heavy books on the base of the ring stand.
7. Place a plastic foam sheet beneath the mass.

Figure 1

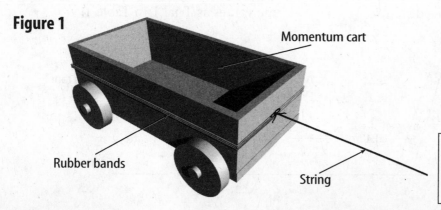

Momentum cart

Rubber bands

String

 SCI 2.e. Students know that when the forces on an object are unbalanced, the object will change its velocity (that is, it will speed up, slow down, or change direction). Also covers **SCI 2.a.**

Laboratory Activity 2 (continued)

Figure 2

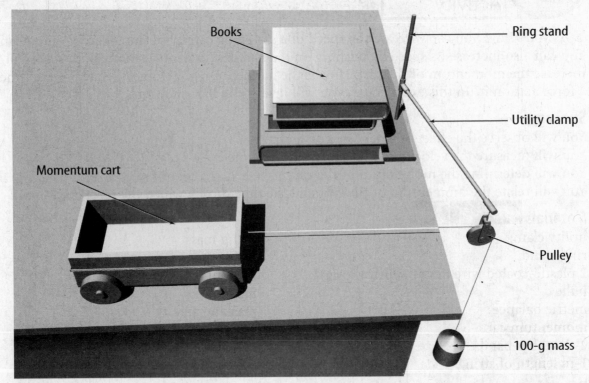

- Books
- Ring stand
- Utility clamp
- Momentum cart
- Pulley
- 100-g mass

8. Pull the cart back until the 100-g mass is about 80 cm above the foam sheet. Have your lab partner place a strip of masking tape on the table marking the position of the front wheels. Release the cart. Observe the motion of the cart. Record your observations on a separate sheet of paper. **CAUTION:** *Have your partner stop the cart before it runs into the pulley.*

9. Using the marker, label the strip of masking tape *Starting Line*. Use the meterstick to measure a distance of 0.20 m from the starting line. Place a strip of masking tape on the table to mark this distance.

Be sure to have the strip of masking tape parallel to the starting line. Label the strip of masking tape *0.20 m*. Measure and label distances of 0.40 m and 0.60 m in the same manner. See Figure 3.

10. Pull the cart back with one hand until its front wheels are on the starting line. Hold the stopwatch in the other hand. Release the cart and immediately start the stopwatch. Measure the time for the front wheels to cross the 0.20-m line. **CAUTION:** *Have your partner stop the cart before it reaches the pulley.* Record the distance and time values as Trial 1 in Table 1.

Figure 3

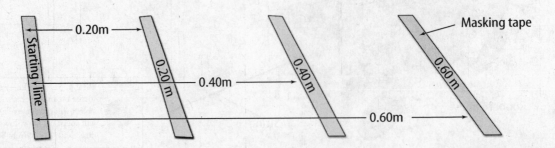

- Starting line
- 0.20m
- 0.20 m
- 0.40m
- 0.40 m
- 0.60m
- 0.60 m
- Masking tape

Laboratory Activity 2 (continued)

11. Repeat step 10 twice. Record the values as Trials 2 and 3.

12. Repeat steps 10 and 11 to measure the time for the front wheels to cross the 0.40-m and 0.60-m lines.

Data and Observations

Table 1

Distance (m)	Time (s)		
	Trial 1	Trial 2	Trial 3

Table 2

Distance (m)	Average time (s)	Average velocity (m/s)	Final velocity (m/s)	Momentum (g·m/s)

Graph 1

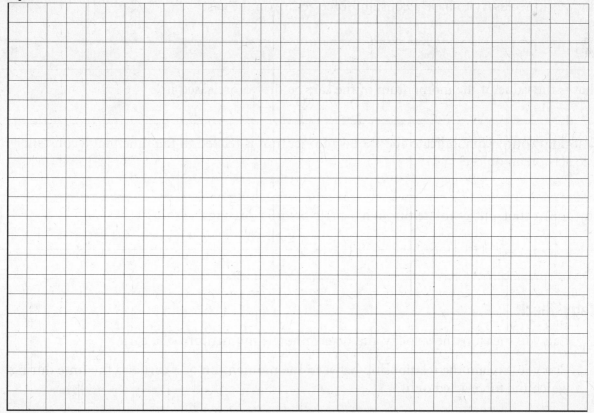

Laboratory Activity 2 (continued)

1. Calculate the average times for the cart to travel 0.20 m, 0.40 m, and 0.60 m. Record these values in Table 2.
2. Calculate the average velocity for each distance by dividing distance traveled by average time. Record these values in Table 2.
3. Because the cart started from rest and had a constant force acting on it, the velocity of the cart at a given distance from the starting line is equal to twice its average velocity for that distance. That is, the velocity of the cart as it crossed the 0.20-m line is twice the value of the average velocity that you calculated for 0.20 m. Calculate the velocity of the cart as it crossed the 0.20-m line, the 0.40-m line, and the 0.60-m line. Record these values in Table 2.
4. Calculate the momentum of the cart as it crossed the 0.20-m, 0.40-m, and 0.60-m lines by multiplying the mass of the cart by its velocity. Record these values in Table 2.
5. Use Graph 1 to make a graph of your data. Plot the average time on the *x*-axis and the momentum on the *y*-axis. Label the *x*-axis *Time (s)* and the *y*-axis *Momentum* (P).

Step 1. Mass of cart: _____ g

Step 8. Observation of motion of a cart:

_____

_____

Questions and Conclusions

1. What force caused the cart to accelerate?

_____

2. Why was it necessary to have a constant force acting on the cart?

_____

_____

3. What is the value of the momentum of the cart before you released it?

_____

4. What does your graph indicate about how momentum is related to the time that a constant force acts on an object?

_____

5. Why does a shot-putter rotate through a circle before releasing the shot?

_____

_____

Strategy Check

_____ Can you measure the velocity and determine the momentum of a cart?

_____ Can you explain the relationship between the momentum of a cart and the time during which the force acted on it?

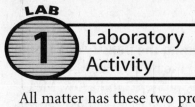

LAB 1 Laboratory Activity — Density of a Liquid

All matter has these two properties – mass and volume. Mass is a measure of the amount of matter. Volume is a measure of the space that the matter occupies. Both mass and volume can be measured using metric units. The standard unit of mass in the SI system is the kilogram (kg). To measure smaller masses, the gram (g) is often used. In the metric system, the volume of a liquid is measured in liters (L) or milliliters (mL). Density is a measure of the amount of matter in a given volume of space. Density may be calculated using the following equation.

$$\text{density} = \frac{\text{mass}}{\text{volume}}$$

Density is a physical property of a liquid. By measuring the mass and volume of a sample of a liquid, the liquid's density can be determined. The density of a liquid is expressed as grams per milliliter (g/mL). For example, the density of distilled water is 1.00 g/mL.

Strategy

You will determine the capacity of a pipette.
You will measure the masses of several liquids.
You will calculate the densities of the liquids.
You will compare the densities of the liquids with that of water.

Materials

4 plastic pipettes
metric balance
distilled water
4 small plastic cups
ethanol
corn oil
corn syrup

> **SCI 8.a.** Students know density is mass per unit volume.
> Also covers **SCI 8.b.**

Procedure

Part A—Determining the Capacity of a Pipette

1. Measure the mass of an empty pipette using the metric balance. Record the mass in the Data and Observations section.
2. Completely fill the bulb of the pipette with distilled water. This can be done as follows:
   a. Pour distilled water into a small plastic cup until it is half full.
   b. Squeeze the bulb of the pipette and insert the stem into the water in the cup.
   c. Draw water into the pipette by releasing pressure on the bulb of the pipette.
   d. Hold the pipette by the bulb with the stem pointed up. Squeeze the bulb slightly to eliminate any air left in the bulb or stem. MAINTAIN PRESSURE ON THE BULB OF THE PIPETTE.

e. Immediately insert the tip of the pipette's stem into the cup of water as shown in Figure.1 Release the pressure on the bulb of the pipette. The pipette will completely fill with water.

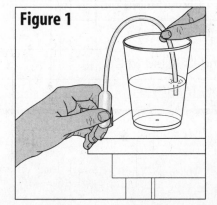

Figure 1

Laboratory Activity 1 (continued)

3. Measure the mass of the water-filled pipette. Record this value in the Data and Observations section.

Part B—Determining the Density of a Liquid

1. Completely fill the bulb of another pipette with ethanol as in Step 2 in Part A. Measure the mass of the ethanol-filled pipette. Record this value in Table 1.

Analysis

1. Calculate the mass of water in the water-filled pipette by subtracting the mass of the empty pipette from the mass of the water-filled pipette. Enter this value in the Data and Observations section.

2. The capacity of the pipette, which is the volume of the fluid that fills the pipette, can be calculated using the density of water. Because the density of water is 1.00 g/mL, a mass of 1 g of water has a volume of 1 mL. Thus, the mass of the water in the pipette is numerically equal to the capacity of the pipette. Enter the capacity of the pipette in the Data and Observations section. Record this value in Table 1 as the volume of liquid for each of the liquids used in Part B.

3. Determine the mass of each liquid by subtracting the mass of the empty pipette from the mass of the liquid-filled pipette. Record the values in Table 1.

4. Using the volumes and the masses of the liquids, calculate their densities and record them in the data table.

Data and Observations

Part A—Determining the Capacity of a Pipette

Mass of empty pipette: _____ g

Mass of water-filled pipette: _____ g

Mass of water: _____ g

Capacity of pipette: _____ mL

Part B—Determining the Density of a Liquid

Table 1

Measurement	Liquid		
	Ethanol	Corn oil	Corn syrup
1. Mass of liquid-filled pipette (g)			
2. Mass of liquid (g)			
3. Volume of liquid (mL)			
4. Density (g/mL)			

Laboratory Activity 1 (continued)

Questions and Conclusions

1. Rank the liquids by their densities starting with the least dense.

_____

_____

2. How does the density of water compare to the densities of the other liquids?

_____

_____

3. What would you observe if you poured corn oil into a beaker of water? Why?

_____

_____

_____

4. The specific gravity of a substance is the ratio of the density of that substance to the density of a standard, which is water. Specific gravity is a measure of the relative density of a substance. Determine the specific gravity of ethanol, corn oil, and corn syrup.

_____

_____

_____

5. Why doesn't specific gravity have units? Determine the specific gravity of ethanol, corn oil, and corn syrup.

_____

_____

_____

Strategy Check

_____ Can you determine the capacity of a pipette?

_____ Can you measure the masses of several liquids?

_____ Can you calculate the densities of the liquids?

_____ Can you compare the densities of the liquids with that of water?

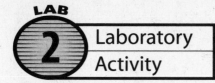

Floating in Freshwater and in Ocean Water

Freshwater and ocean water (salt water) have several different physical and chemical properties. One of the properties in which they differ influences how well an object floats. Both freshwater and salt water exert a buoyant force on a floating object.

Strategy

You will compare a boat floating in freshwater with a boat floating in salt water.
You will determine the relationship between the density of a liquid and its buoyant force.
You will observe how salt water and freshwater mix.

Materials

10 cm × 10 cm aluminum foil
25-mL graduated cylinder
clear-plastic storage boxes (2)
ocean water (salt water—make solution with salt and water)
freshwater (aged tap water)
grease pencil
metric ruler
50-mL beaker (2)
balance
food coloring
dropper
colored pencils

Procedure

1. Fold the square of aluminum foil into a boat as shown in Figure 1.
2. Half fill one plastic box with salt water. Half fill the other plastic box with freshwater.
3. Float the aluminum boat in the salt water. Mark the waterline on the boat using the grease pencil. Measure the distance from the bottom of the boat to the waterline. Record in Table 1.

4. Float the same aluminum boat in the freshwater. Mark the waterline again.
5. Measure from the bottom of the boat to the new waterline and record.
6. Pour 25 mL of salt water into a beaker. Determine the mass of the salt water. Record the volume and mass in Table 1.
7. Pour 25 mL of freshwater into the second beaker. Determine the mass of the freshwater and record its volume and mass.
8. Color the salt water using food coloring.
9. Using the dropper, add freshwater to the beaker until you see a layer of freshwater on top of the salt water. NOTE: Allow the freshwater to run slowly down the inside wall of the beaker so it does not disturb the salt water. Sketch the layers in the beaker in Table 1.
10. Allow the beaker to stand undisturbed for several days, then observe the results. Sketch the results in Table 1.

SCI 8.c. Students know the buoyant force on an object in a fluid is an upward force equal to the weight of the fluid the object has displaced. Also covers **SCI 8.d.**

Figure 1

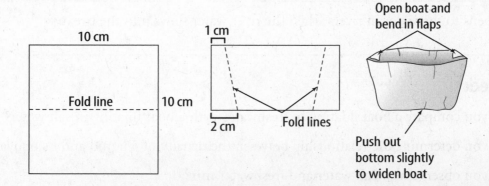

Laboratory Activity 2 (continued)

Data and Observations

Table 1

	Mass (g)	Volume (cm³)	Depth of Waterline (cm)
Salt Water			
Freshwater			
Beaker (start)		Beaker (after several days)	

Questions and Conclusions

1. In which liquid does the boat float higher? _____

2. State a hypothesis to explain your answer.

   _____

   _____

3. Defend your hypothesis with what you observed about the waterline for each boat.

   _____

4. Why are you able to add a layer of water on top of the salt water?

   _____

5. State the relationship between the density of a liquid and its buoyant force.

   _____

6. Does this confirm or contradict your hypothesis? Explain.

   _____

7. What can happen to two liquids with different densities if they are in contact over a long period of time?

   _____

8. What happens to the water in rivers when the river water flows into the ocean?

   _____

Strategy Check

_____ Can you compare a boat floating in freshwater with a boat floating in salt water?

_____ Can you determine the relationship between the density of a liquid and its buoyant force?

_____ Can you observe how salt water and freshwater mix?

Chemical Bonds

LAB 1 — Laboratory Activity

An ion is an atom that is no longer neutral because it has gained or lost electrons. One important property of ions is the ability to conduct electricity in solution.

Ions can form in solution in several ways. Ionic compounds, which are often compounds created from metals of Groups 1 and 2 and nonmetals in Groups 16 and 17, dissolve in water to form ions. Acids and bases also form ions in solution. Although acids and bases contain covalent bonds (bonds in which electrons are shared), acids form the hydronium ion (H_3O^+), while bases form the hydroxide ion (OH^-) in water.

Other covalent compounds form solutions, too. These solutions, however, do not conduct an electric current because they do not form ions in solution. A measure of how well a solution can carry an electric current is called conductivity.

Strategy

You will determine the conductivity of several solutions.

You will classify the compounds that were dissolved in the solutions as ionic compounds or covalent compounds.

Materials

9-V battery and battery clip
tape
cardboard sheet, 10 cm × 10 cm
alligator clips (4)
LED (light-emitting diode)
resistor, 1,000-Ω
copper wire, insulated, 20-cm lengths (2)
microplate, 24-well
pipettes, plastic (7)
sulfuric acid solution, $0.1M\ H_2SO_4$
sodium chloride solution, $0.1M\ NaCl$
sodium hydroxide solution, $0.1M\ NaOH$
sucrose solution, $0.1M$ sucrose
glucose solution, $0.1M$ glucose
sugar cubes (sucrose)
sodium chloride (rock, crystalline)
water, distilled
paper towels
WARNING: *Sulfuric acid and sodium hydroxide can cause burns. Avoid contacting them with your skin or clothing. Do not taste, eat, or drink any materials used in the lab.*

Procedure

Part A—Constructing a Conductivity Tester

1. After putting your apron and goggles on, attach the 9-V battery clip to the 9-V battery. Use tape to attach the battery securely to the cardboard sheet, as shown in Figure 1.
2. Attach an alligator clip to one of the lead wires of the 1,000-Ω resistor. Connect the alligator clip to the *red* lead wire of the battery clip. Tape the resistor and alligator clip to the cardboard sheet as shown in Figure 2. **WARNING:** *Use care when handling sharp objects.*
3. Attach an alligator clip to the *long* lead wire of the LED. Connect this alligator clip to the second wire of the 1,000-Ω resistor. Tape the alligator clip to the cardboard sheet.
4. Attach an alligator clip to the *short* lead wire of the LED. Connect this clip to one end of one of the insulated copper wires. Tape the clip to the cardboard sheet as shown in Figure 3.
5. Attach the last alligator clip to one end of the second insulated copper wire. Connect the alligator clip to the *black* lead wire of the battery clip. Tape the alligator clip to the cardboard sheet as shown in Figure 4.
6. Check to be certain that the alligator clips, resistor, and battery are securely taped to the cardboard sheet and that the clips are not touching one another.

SCI 3.a. Students know the structure of the atom and know it is composed of protons, neutrons, and electrons.

Laboratory Activity 1 (continued)

7. Have your teacher check your conductivity tester.

8. Touch the two ends of the two insulated wires and observe that the LED glows.

Figure 1

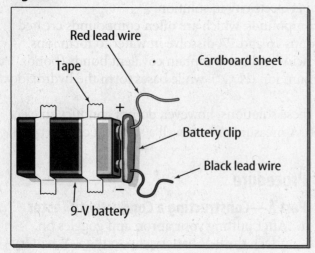

Red lead wire

Tape

Cardboard sheet

Battery clip

Black lead wire

9-V battery

Figure 3

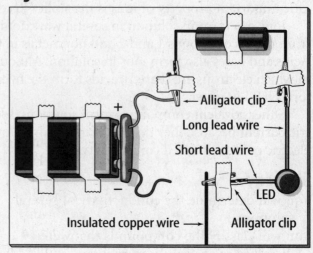

Alligator clip

Long lead wire

Short lead wire

Insulated copper wire

LED

Alligator clip

Figure 2

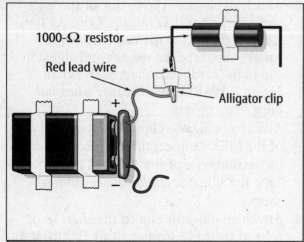

1000-Ω resistor

Red lead wire

Alligator clip

Figure 4

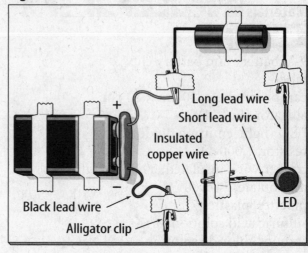

Long lead wire

Short lead wire

Insulated copper wire

Black lead wire

Alligator clip

LED

Laboratory Activity 1 (continued)

Figure 5

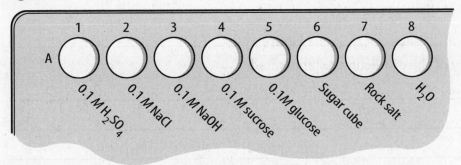

Part B—Testing the Conductivity of a Solution

1. Place the microplate on a flat surface. Have the numbered columns of the microplate at the top and the lettered rows at the left. **WARNING:** *Wash hands immediately after coming in contact with any of the prepared solutions. Inform your teacher if you come in contact with any chemicals.*

2. Using a clean pipette, add a pipette of the sulfuric acid solution to well A1.

3. Using another clean pipette, add a pipette of the sodium chloride solution to well A2.

4. Repeat step 3 for each remaining solution. Use a clean pipette for each solution. Add the sodium hydroxide solution to well A3, the sucrose solution to well A4, the glucose solution to well A5, a sugar cube to well A6, and a piece of rock salt to well A7.

5. Using a clean pipette, add a pipette of distilled water to well A8. For steps 1–5 see Figure 5.

6. Place the exposed ends of the two insulated copper wires into the solution in well A1, positioning the wires so they are at opposite sides of the well. Be sure that the exposed ends of the wire are completely submerged.

7. Observe the LED. Use the brightness of the LED as an indication of the conductivity of the solution. Rate the conductivity of the solution using the following symbols: + (good conductivity); – (fair conductivity); or 0 (no conductivity). Record your rating in the corresponding well of the microplate shown in Figure 6.

8. Remove the wires and dry the ends of the wires with a paper towel.

9. Repeat steps 6, 7, and 8 for each remaining well in the microplate.

Data and Observations

Figure 6

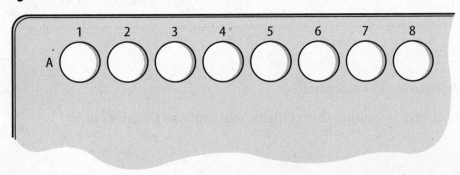

Laboratory Activity 1 (continued)

Questions and Conclusions

1. What is the conductivity of distilled water?

_____

2. Why was the conductivity of the distilled water measured?

_____

_____

_____

3. After studying your results, infer which solutions contained ions. Which solutions did not contain ions?

_____

_____

4. Which solutions contained covalent compounds? Did any of these solutions conduct an electric current?

_____

_____

5. Did the crystal of table salt or the sugar cube conduct electricity?

_____

_____

6. How did the conductivities of the crystal of table salt and the 0.1M NaCl solution compare?

_____

_____

7. From your results, describe one property of ions in solution.

_____

_____

Strategy Check

_____ Can you test the conductivity of a solution?

_____ Can you distinguish between a solution that contains ions and one that does not?

Isotopes and Atomic Mass

Elements as they occur in nature are mixtures of isotopes. All the isotopes of any given element have the same number of protons, but each isotope has a different number of neutrons. Most elements have more than one isotope. Therefore, the atomic masses of elements that are included in the periodic table are average atomic masses. In this exercise, you will use a model of isotopes to help you understand the concept of average atomic mass.

Strategy

You will model isotopes of two different elements using candy-coated peanuts and candy-coated chocolate in two colors.

You will determine the average mass of the two colors of candy-coated peanuts and candy-coated chocolate.

You will relate your results to the average atomic mass of elements.

Materials

4 red and 3 green candy-coated peanuts
4 red and 3 green candy-coated chocolates

Procedure

1. Group together four red candy-coated peanuts and two red candy-coated chocolates. The two different kinds of candy represent two isotopes of the same element.

2. Assume that a red peanut has a mass of 2 candy units, and a red chocolate has a mass of 1 candy unit. Calculate the average mass of the red candy as follows:

   a. Calculate the total mass of red peanuts by multiplying the number of red peanuts by the mass of one peanut candy.

   b. Calculate the total mass of red chocolates by multiplying the number of red chocolates by the mass of one chocolate candy.

   c. Add these two total masses together and divide by the total number of candies.

3. Repeat step 2 using three green peanuts and three green chocolates. Assume a green peanut has a mass of 4 units and a green chocolate has a mass of 3 units.

4. Record your calculations in the table in the Data and Observations section.

Data and Observations

	Mass of peanuts (number of candies × mass of 1 unit)	Mass of Chocolates (number of candies × mass of 1 unit)	Average mass (total mass / total number of candies)
Red			
Green			

SCI 7.b. Students know each element has a specific number of protons in the nucleus (the atomic number) and each isotope of the element has a different but specific number of neutrons in the nucleus.

Laboratory Activity 2 (continued)

Questions and Conclusions

1. There were six red and six green candies. Why were their calculated average masses different?

_____

_____

_____

_____

2. Calculate the average mass of Y in a sample of element Y that contains 100 atoms of Y-12 and 10 atoms of Y-14.

3. Look at the atomic masses of elements in the periodic table. Notice that none of the atomic masses of naturally abundant elements are whole numbers. Use your candy model of atoms to explain this.

_____

_____

_____

_____

4. Uranium is an element used in most nuclear reactors. Its two major isotopes are U-235 and U-238. Look up the mass of uranium on the periodic table. Infer which isotope is the most common, and explain why you came to this conclusion.

_____

_____

_____

_____

5. Compare and contrast mass number and average atomic mass.

_____

_____

_____

_____

Laboratory Activity 2 (continued)

6. Hydrogen has three isotopes. The most common one, protium, has no neutrons. Deuterium, the second isotope, has one neutron. Tritium has two neutrons. Using this information, calculate the mass number of these isotopes.

_____

_____

_____

_____

Strategy Check

_____ Can you explain how candy-coated peanuts and candy-coated chocolate can be used as a model for isotopes?

_____ Are you able to find the average mass of an element?

LAB 1 Laboratory Activity

Mixtures and Compounds

Matter is anything that has mass and occupies space. Matter exists in different forms. Three classifications of matter are well known to us: elements, mixtures, and compounds. Elements are the basic materials of our world. Elements in a mixture have recognizable boundaries and can be separated by mechanical means. Elements that form a chemical compound can be separated only by a chemical process. The element oxygen(O) combines with the element hydrogen (H) to form water (H_2O), which is a compound. Salt water is a mixture of two compounds, water and salt.

Strategy

You will separate a mixture into its parts.
You will compare the characteristics of a compound and a mixture.

Materials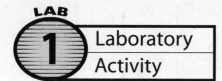

magnifying glass
sand (coarse)
granite rock
granite (crushed)

water
disposable pie pans (2)
rock salt
heat source

Procedure

1. Use the magnifying glass to observe the sand and granite rock. Sketch the granite with the minerals in it, and the shapes of the sand grains under Sketch A.
2. Sort the crushed granite into separate piles according to color.
3. Sketch the general shape of a piece from each pile of the sorted granite, and label each as to color under Sketch B.
4. Mix a spoonful of sand in some water in a pie pan. Sketch what you observed under Sketch C.

5. Examine and sketch the salt crystals under Sketch D. **WARNING:** *Do not ingest rock salt. It might contain harmful impurities.*
6. Mix a spoonful of salt in some water in the second pie pan. Record your observations.
7. Heat both pans until the water is evaporated. Sketch what is left in each pan under Sketch E. **WARNING:** *Be careful not to get clothes or hair close to the heat source.*

Data and Observations

Sketch A

Sketch B

 SCI 3.b. Students know that compounds are formed by combining two or more different elements and that compounds have properties that are different from their constituent elements. Also covers **SCI 7.c.**

Laboratory Activity 1 (continued)

Sketch C

Sketch D

Sketch E

Questions and Conclusions

1. Are any of the sand grains similar to any of the granite fragments? If so, describe them.

_____

_____

2. How are salt and sand similar? How are they different?

_____

_____

3. Is salt water a compound or a mixture? Explain.

_____

_____

4. Is granite a compound or a mixture? Explain.

_____

_____

5. Name some mechanical processes used to separate mixtures.

_____

_____

Strategy Check

_____ Can you separate components of a mixture?

_____ Can you tell the difference between a compound and a mixture?

Constructing Compounds

All elements are made of atoms. Compounds are formed when two or more elements combine to form a different type of matter. A chemical formula is a shortcut chemists take to describe a specific compound. It tells the numbers and types of atoms that make up a single unit of a compound. You probably already know that the formula for one common compound—water—is H_2O. The formula for water tells us that a molecule of water has two hydrogen atoms and one oxygen atom.

Strategy

You will build models of different compounds.
You will use your models to determine how many atoms of each element are in each molecule.

Materials

modeling clay (red, yellow, and blue)
toothpicks

Procedure

1. Obtain enough clay to make four balls of each color. Each clay ball represents one atom of an element. Blue balls represent hydrogen atoms, red balls represent oxygen atoms, and yellow balls represent carbon atoms.

2. Using toothpicks to connect your clay atoms as shown Figure 1, construct a model of each of the following compounds. After you construct each model, fill in the blanks for that compound in the table in the Data and Observations section. After you finish making the molecules for water and carbon dioxide, take them apart. Then make the methane molecule.

   Figure 1

   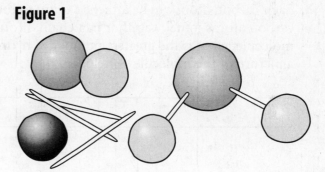

   a. H_2O (water): Connect two hydrogen atoms to one oxygen atom.

   b. CO_2 (carbon dioxide): Connect two oxygen atoms to one carbon atom.

   c. CH_4 (methane): Connect four hydrogen atoms to one carbon atom.

SCI 3.b. Students know that compounds are formed by combining two or more different elements and that compounds have properties that are different from their constituent elements.

Laboratory Activity 2 (continued)

Data and Observations

Chemical formula	Number of atoms in compound			
	Hydrogen	Carbon	Oxygen	Total
1. H_2O (water)				
2. CO_2 (carbon dioxide)				
3. CH_4 (methane)				

Questions and Conclusions

1. What would the answers in the table be for a molecule of fruit sugar, $C_6H_{12}O_6$?

_____

2. From the formulas given, identify each of the following as either an element or a compound: NaCl, Ag, Co, CO, SO_2, AgBr.

_____

_____

3. Each carbon atom can be attached to up to four other atoms. The compound hexane has six carbon atoms joined together in a chain. If only carbon and hydrogen make up the hexane molecule, what is the greatest number of hydrogen atoms that could be in the molecule? Draw a picture of the molecule to help you.

_____

_____

4. Nitrogen in air is in the form of two nitrogen atoms fastened together, N_2. Is nitrogen an element or is it a compound? Explain.

_____

_____

Strategy Check

_____ Can you make a simple model of a compound based on its molecular formula?

_____ Based on a compound's molecular formula, can you figure out how many atoms of each element are in a compound?

_____ Do you understand the difference between an element and a compound?

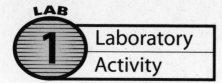

States of Matter

LAB 1 Laboratory Activity

Three common states of matter are solid, liquid, and gas. A fourth state of matter, the plasma state, exists only at extremely high temperatures. Differences among the physical states depend on the attractions between the atoms or molecules and on the rate of movement of the atoms or molecules. Pressure and temperature control these two factors.

Strategy

You will observe the characteristics of a solid.
You will change a gas to a liquid.
You will compare the characteristics of a solid, a liquid, and a gas.

> **SCI 3.d.** Students know the states of matter (solid, liquid, gas) depend on molecular motion. Also covers **SCI 5.d.**

Materials

marker
beaker (1,000-mL)
ice cubes (frozen from 500 mL of water)

ice cube tray
plastic drinking glass (cold or add an ice cube)
water

Procedure

1. Mark the level of the top of the ice cubes while they are still in the tray. Remove the ice cubes and place them in the beaker. Record the characteristics of ice in Table 1.

2. Let the ice cubes melt. Record the characteristics of the resulting water in Table 1.

3. Pour the water back into the tray. Mark the level of the top of the water on the tray.

Under "Other characteristics" in Table 1, record whether this level is higher or lower than that of the ice.

4. Place the cold glass in a warm area. After a few minutes, record your observations of the surface of the glass in Table 1.

5. Place an ice cube in the beaker of water. Observe whether or not it floats. Record your observations in Table 1.

Data and Observations

Table 1

Material	State of matter	Takes shape of container (yes or no)	Other characteristics
Ice cubes			floats: yes or no
Water			higher or lower in tray than ice

Material	Observations
Glass	
Beaker with ice	

Laboratory Activity 1 (continued)

Questions and Conclusions

1. What is solid water called?

_____

Liquid water?

_____

Water as a gas?

_____

2. Did the ice cube sink or float in the water? Explain.

_____

_____

3. Which occupies more volume, an equal amount of water or ice? Explain.

_____

_____

4. Where did the water on the glass come from?

_____

What are the characteristics of water as a gas?

_____

5. What change caused the water vapor to change to a liquid?

_____

_____

6. If you changed liquid water to water vapor in a pressure cooker, what volume would the water vapor occupy?

_____

7. Compare the characteristics of water as a solid, a liquid, and a gas.

_____

_____

_____

Strategy Check

_____ Can you observe the characteristics of a solid?

_____ Can you observe a gas change to a liquid?

_____ Can you compare the characteristics of a solid, a liquid, and a gas?

2 LAB Laboratory Activity

The Behavior of Gases

Because most gases are colorless, odorless, and tasteless, we tend to forget that gases are matter. Because the molecules of a gas are far apart and free to move, a gas fills its container. The volume of a gas changes with changes in its temperature and pressure. Gases expand and contract as the pressure on them changes. Gases expand when the pressure on them decreases. They contract when the pressure on them increases. The volume and pressure of a gas are inversely related. Gases also expand and contract as their temperature changes. The expansion of a gas varies directly with its temperature.

Strategy

You will observe how the volume of a gas is affected by a change in pressure.
You will observe how the volume of a gas is affected by a change in temperature.

Materials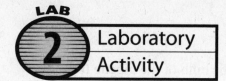

methylene blue solution
3 small plastic cups
2 plastic microtip pipettes
water
hot plate, laboratory burner,
   or immersion heater

pliers
5 identical books
metric ruler
24-well microplate

iron or lead washer
masking tape
250-mL beaker

Procedure

Part A—Volume and Pressure of a Gas

1. Place two drops of methylene blue solution in a small plastic cup. Pour water into the cup until it is half full.

2. Fill only the bulb of the plastic pipette with this solution.

3. Seal the tip of the pipette in the following manner: Soften the tip of the pipette by holding the tip near the surface of the hot plate or near the flame of the burner. **WARNING:** *Do not place the tip of the stem on the hot plate or in the flame of the burner. Avoid coming in contact with the hot plate or the flame of the burner.* Away from the heat, squeeze the softened tip of the pipette with the pliers to seal the end. See Figure 1.

4. Place one of the books on the bulb of the pipette and measure in mm the length of the column of air trapped in the stem of the pipette. Record this value in Table 1.

5. Predict what will happen to the length of the trapped air column if another book is placed on top of the first book. Record your prediction in the Data and Observations section.

6. Place another book on top of the first book. Measure, in mm, the length of the column of trapped air and record the measure in Table 1.

7. Continue adding books one at a time, until five books are stacked on top of the pipette. After adding each book, measure the length of the column of trapped air and record the measurement in Table 1.

Figure 1

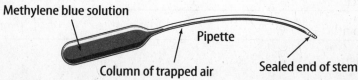

Methylene blue solution

Pipette

Column of trapped air

Sealed end of stem

 SCI 3.d. Students know the states of matter (solid, liquid, gas) depend on molecular motion. Also covers **SCI 3.e.**

Copyright © Glencoe/McGraw-Hill, a division of The McGraw-Hill Companies, Inc.

Laboratory Activity 2 (continued)

Part B—Volume and Temperature of a Gas

1. Fill a well of the microplate with water. Add a few drops of methylene blue solution to the well.

2. Place an iron or lead washer over the end of the stem of the second pipette. Place the bulb in a plastic cup two-thirds filled with water at room temperature. See Figure 2.

Figure 2

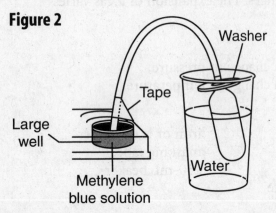

Washer

Tape

Large well

Methylene blue solution

Water

3. Bend the stem of the pipette into the solution in the well of the microplate. With the tip of the stem below the surface of the solution, tape the stem to the side of the microplate. The tip of the stem must remain below the surface of the solution during the remainder of the experiment. See Figure 2.

4. Predict what you will observe if the bulb of the pipette is gently heated. Write your prediction in the Data and Observations section.

5. Heat some water in the 250-mL beaker to a temperature of 30° C.

6. Pour the warmed water into another plastic cup until it is two-thirds full.

7. Remove the bulb of the pipette from the room-temperature water and place it in the warm water in the second cup. Immediately begin counting the bubbles that rise from the tip of the stem submerged in the well of the microplate until it stops bubbling. Record the number of bubbles and the temperature of the water in Table 2.

8. Empty the water from the first plastic cup.

9. Add some water to the beaker and heat the water to a temperature of 35° C. Pour this water into the first plastic cup until it is two-thirds full.

10. Remove the bulb of the pipette from the second cup and place it in the water in the first cup. Count the number of bubbles that rise in the well of the microplate. Record this number and the temperature of the water in Table 2. Empty the water from the second plastic cup.

11. Repeat steps 8–10 for the water that has been heated to 40°C, 45°C, and 50°C .

Analysis

1. Make a graph of your data from Part A using Graph 1. Plot the pressure on the x-axis and the length of the trapped air column on the y-axis. Label the x-axis *Pressure (books)* and the y-axis *Length (mm)*.

2. Complete the third column of Table 2. Make a graph of your data from Part B using Graph 2. Plot the temperature on the x-axis and the total number of bubbles on the y-axis. Label the x-axis *Temperature (°C)* and the y-axis *Total number of bubbles*.

Data and Observations

Part A—Volume and Pressure of a Gas

1. Prediction of length of trapped air column if the pressure on the pipette bulb is increased:

_____

_____

Laboratory Activity 2 (continued)

Table 1

Pressure (number of books)	Length of column of trapped air (mm)
1	
2	
3	
4	
5	

Part B—Volume and Temperature of a Gas

2. Prediction of observations if the air in the bubble is heated:

_____

_____

Graph 1

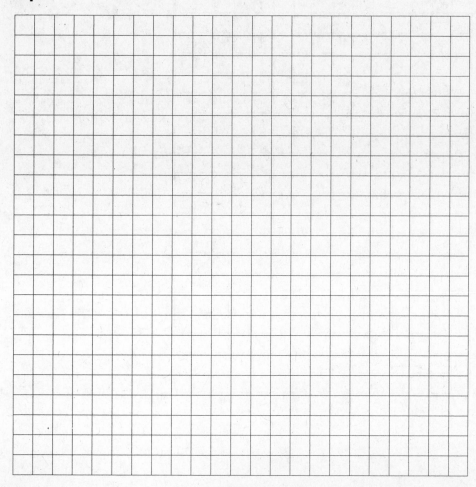

Laboratory Activity 2 (continued)

Table 2

Temperature (˚C)	Number of bubbles	Total number of bubbles
_____ (room temp)		
30		
35		
40		
45		
50		

Graph 2

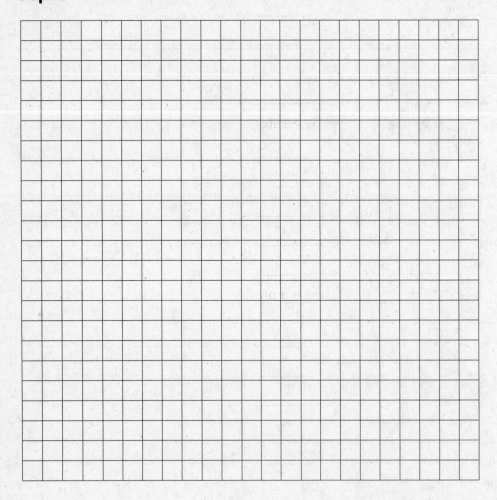

Laboratory Activity 2 (continued)

Questions and Conclusions

1. Explain how the change in the length of the column of trapped air in Part A is a measure of the change in the volume of the air trapped in the pipette.

_____

_____

_____

_____

_____

2. Why did you have to stack identical books on the bulb of the pipette?

_____

_____

_____

_____

_____

3. What is the relationship between the volume and pressure of a gas?

_____

_____

_____

_____

_____

4. Explain why the total number of bubbles produced is a measure of the change in volume of the air that was heated in the bulb of the pipette.

_____

_____

_____

_____

_____

Laboratory Activity 2 (continued)

5. Use your graph to predict the total number of bubbles released if the bulb of the pipette were placed in water at a temperature of 60°C.

_____

_____

6. During each 5°C temperature change, the number of bubbles released was the same. What does this indicate?

_____

_____

_____

7. What is the relationship between the volume and temperature of a gas?

_____

_____

_____

Strategy Check

_____ Can you observe how the volume of a gas is affected by a change in pressure?

_____ Can you observe how the volume of a gas is affected by a change in temperature?

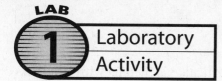

Relationships Among Elements

SCI 7.a. Students know how to identify regions corresponding to metals, nonmetals, and inert gases. Also covers **SCI 7.c.**

The periodic table is a wonderful source of information about all of the elements scientists have discovered. In this activity, you will investigate the relationship among the elements' atomic numbers, radii, and positions in the periodic table.

An atom's atomic radius is the distance from the center of the nucleus to the edge of the atom. The radii for elements with atomic numbers from 3 through 38 are given in Table 1. The radii are so small that a very small metric unit called a picometer is used. A picometer (pm) is one trillionth of a meter.

Strategy

You will plot the atomic radii of elements with atomic numbers 3 through 38.
You will examine the graph for repeated patterns.

Materials

copy of the periodic table   graph paper   pencil

Table 1

Name and symbol		Atomic number	Atomic radius (picometers)	Name and symbol		Atomic number	Atomic radius (picometers)
Aluminum	Al	13	143	Magnesium	Mg	12	160
Argon	Ar	18	98	Manganese	Mn	25	127
Arsenic	As	33	120	Neon	Ne	10	71
Beryllium	Be	4	112	Nickel	Ni	28	124
Boron	B	5	85	Nitrogen	N	7	75
Bromine	Br	35	114	Oxygen	O	8	73
Calcium	Ca	20	197	Phosphorus	P	15	110
Carbon	C	6	77	Potassium	K	19	227
Chlorine	Cl	17	100	Rubidium	Rb	37	248
Chromium	Cr	24	128	Scandium	Sc	21	162
Cobalt	Co	27	125	Selenium	Se	34	119
Copper	Cu	29	128	Silicon	Si	14	118
Fluorine	F	9	72	Sodium	Na	11	186
Gallium	Ga	31	135	Strontium	Sr	38	215
Germanium	Ge	32	122	Sulfur	S	16	103
Iron	Fe	26	126	Titanium	Ti	22	147
Krypton	Kr	36	112	Vanadium	V	23	134
Lithium	Li	3	152	Zinc	Zn	30	134

Laboratory Activity 1 (continued)

Procedure

1. On the graph paper, label the horizontal axis with the numbers 0 through 38 to represent the atomic numbers of the elements you will be plotting.

2. Label the vertical axis by tens with numbers from 0 through 280. These numbers represent atomic radii.

3. Plot the atomic radius for each of the elements with atomic numbers 3 through 38.

Questions and Conclusions

1. Look at the shape of your graph. What patterns do you observe?

_____

2. What family is represented by the high peaks in your graph? _____

3. What family is represented by the low points in your graph? _____

4. What family is represented by the smaller peaks just before the high peaks? _____

5. What do you notice about the radii of the elements at the high peaks as you move from left to right on your graph? Look at your periodic table and find the element that represents each high peak. What does each high peak begin in the periodic table?

_____

_____

6. What happens to the radii of the elements between two highest peaks? What does each of these groups of elements represent?

_____

_____

7. How can a graph such as the one you made help to predict the properties of elements that have not been discovered yet?

_____

_____

_____

8. How do the radii of metals in each period compare with the radii of nonmetals in that period?

_____

Strategy Check

_____ Can you plot a graph of the atomic radii of elements?

_____ Can you observe repeating patterns in the graph?

Periodicity

LAB 2 Laboratory Activity

A periodic event is one that occurs time after time in a regular, predictable way. If you have a table of repeating events, you can use it to predict what might be true in the future. For example, astronomers are able to predict the appearance of a comet if they know the dates of the comet's appearance in the past. A calendar is a good model for the periodic table of the elements.

Strategy

You will determine missing information on the calendar for a month.
You will make predictions about future and past events based on the calendar.

Procedure

1. Label the seven columns of the calendar page in Figure 1 with the numbers 1 through 7. There are seven families, or groups, in this periodic table. They are the days of the week.

2. Label the five rows of the calendar page with the numbers 1 through 5. There are five periods in this periodic table. Each period is a week.

3. Notice that some information is missing. Fill in the missing information by examining the information in the blocks surrounding the spots where the missing information belongs.

Data and Observations

Figure 1

SUN	MON	TUE	WED	THUR	FRI	SAT
				1	2	3 Soccer practice
4	5	6	7	8	9	10
11	12	@	#	15	16	17 Soccer practice
18	19	20	21	22	23	24
25	26	27	28	29	30 Your Birthday	31

 SCI 7.a. Students know how to identify regions corresponding to metals, nonmetals, and inert gases.

Laboratory Activity 2 (continued)

Questions and Conclusions

1. Two of the days in Families 3 and 4 are marked with an @ and a #. What dates should go in these positions?

   _____

2. Family 5 doesn't have a name. What is the correct name for this family?

   _____

3. What dates are included in the third period of the table?

   _____

4. Assuming that the previous month had 30 days, what day of the week would the 28th of that month have been?

   _____

5. What period of this table would it appear in?

   _____

6. Notice that two dates have been scheduled for regular soccer practice. When would you expect the next two soccer practices to take place?

   _____

7. The following month will start on the day after the 31st. What day of the week will it be?

   _____

8. Suppose your birthday occurs on the 30th of the month. Explain how your birthday is a periodic event.

   _____

Strategy Check

_____ Can you provide missing information in a periodic table if you have information about the neighboring blocks?

_____ Can you make predictions based upon information in a periodic table?

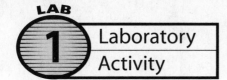

Conservation of Mass

LAB 1 Laboratory Activity

In a chemical reaction, the total mass of the substances formed by the reaction is equal to the total mass of the substances that reacted. This principle is called the law of conservation of mass, which states that matter is not created or destroyed during a chemical reaction.

In this experiment, sodium hydrogen carbonate, $NaHCO_3$ (baking soda), will react with hydrochloric acid, HCl. The substances formed by this reaction are sodium chloride, NaCl; water, H_2O; and carbon dioxide gas, CO_2.

Strategy

You will show that new substances are formed in a chemical reaction.
You will show the conservation of mass during a chemical reaction.

Materials

sealable plastic sandwich bag containing sodium hydrogen carbonate, $NaHCO_3$
hydrochloric acid, HCl 1*M*
plastic pipette
paper towel
metric balance

Procedure

1. Obtain the plastic sandwich bag containing a small amount of sodium hydrogen carbonate.

2. Fill the pipette with the hydrochloric acid solution. Use a paper towel to wipe away any acid that might be on the outside of the pipette. Discard the paper towel.
   WARNING: *Hydrochloric acid is corrosive. Handle with care.*

Figure 1

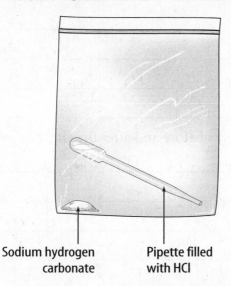

Sodium hydrogen carbonate

Pipette filled with HCl

3. Carefully place the pipette in the bag. Press the bag gently to eliminate as much air as possible. Be careful not to press the bulb of the pipette. Seal the bag. See Figure 1.

4. Measure the mass of the sealed plastic bag using the metric balance. Record this value in the Data and Observations section.

5. Remove the plastic bag from the balance. Without opening the bag, direct the stem of the pipette into the sodium hydrogen carbonate. Press the bulb of the pipette and allow the hydrochloric acid to react with the sodium hydrogen carbonate. Make sure that all the acid mixes with the sodium hydrogen carbonate.

6. Observe the contents of the bag for several minutes. Record your observations in the Data and Observations section.

7. After several minutes, measure the mass of the sealed plastic bag and its contents. Record this value in the Data and Observations section.

SCI 5.b. Students know the idea of atoms explains the conservation of matter: In chemical reactions the number of atoms stays the same no matter how they are arranged, so their total mass stays the same.

Laboratory Activity 1 (continued)

Data and Observations

Table 1

Mass of plastic bag before reaction (in grams)	
Observations from Step 6	
Mass of plastic bag after reaction (in grams)	

Questions and Conclusions

1. Why was it important for the plastic bag to be sealed?

_____

_____

_____

_____

_____

2. What did you observe that indicated that a chemical reaction took place?

_____

_____

_____

_____

3. Compare the mass of the plastic bag and its contents before and after the chemical reaction.

_____

_____

_____

_____

Laboratory Activity 1 (continued)

4. Does your comparison in Question 3 confirm the conservation of mass during this chemical reaction? Explain.

_____

_____

_____

_____

_____

Strategy Check

_____ Can you demonstrate that new substances are formed in a chemical reaction?

_____ Can you show the conservation of mass during a chemical reaction?

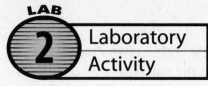

Chemical Reactions

LAB 2 Laboratory Activity

The changes that occur during a chemical reaction are represented by a chemical equation. An equation uses chemical symbols to represent the substances that change. The reactants, on the left side of the equation, are the substances that react. The products, on the right side of the equation, are the substances that are formed from the reaction.

In the following reaction, two reactants form one product. Water and oxygen are the reactants. The product is hydrogen peroxide.

$$H_2O + \frac{1}{2}O_2 \rightarrow H_2O_2$$

A chemical reaction may have two products from the breakdown of a single reactant. In this example water is the reactant. Hydrogen and oxygen are products.

$$2H_2O \rightarrow 2H_2 + O_2$$

Two reactants can also combine to make two products. In the following reaction, carbon displaces the hydrogen in water and hydrogen and carbon monoxide are released as gases.

$$H_2O + C \rightarrow H_2 + CO$$

Strategy

You will recognize the reactants and products of a chemical reaction.
You will write a word equation for a chemical reaction.
You will write a balanced chemical equation using chemical symbols.

SCI 5.a. Students know reactant atoms and molecules interact to form products with different chemical properties. Also covers **SCI 5.c.**

Materials

Part A	Part B	Part C
aluminum foil	matches	common nail, Fe
burner	test tube	steel wool
matches	spoon	string
tongs	baking soda, $NaHCO_3$	beaker
steel wool	wood splint	copper (II) sulfate solution, $CuSO_4$
	hot water bath	watch or clock
		paper towel

WARNING: *Copper (II) sulfate solution is poisonous. Handle with care. Wear goggles and an apron.*

Procedure

Part A—Two Reactants→One Product

1. Observe the color of the steel wool. Record your observations in the Data and Observations section.

2. Predict changes in the steel wool when it is heated in the flame. Write your prediction in the Data and Observations section.

3. Protect the table with a sheet of aluminum foil. Place the burner in the center of the foil. Light the burner. **WARNING:** *Stay clear of flames.*

Figure 1

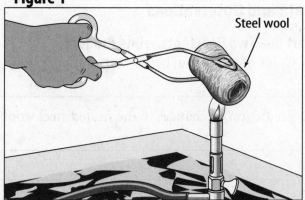

Steel wool

Laboratory Activity 2 (continued)

4. Hold the steel wool (containing iron, Fe) with the tongs over the flame as shown in Figure 1. As the steel wool burns, record the changes it goes through.

Part B—One Reactant→Two Products

1. Set up a hot water bath.
2. Place a spoonful of baking soda, $NaHCO_3$, in a test tube. Place the test tube in the hot water bath. Do not point the mouth of the test tube toward anyone. In the Data and Observations section, write your prediction of what will happen as the baking soda is heated.
3. Record the description and colors of the products formed inside the tube as it is heated.
4. Test for the presence of CO_2. Light a wood splint. Insert the flaming splint into the mouth of the test tube, as shown in Figure 2. If the flame of the splint goes out, CO_2 is present. Record your observations of the products of this reaction.

Part C—Two Reactants→Two Products

1. Carefully rub the nail with a piece of steel wool until the nail is shiny. Tie a string around the nail. Fill a beaker about half full with the $CuSO_4$ solution. Record the colors of the nail and the $CuSO_4$ solution in Table 1.
   WARNING: *Use care when handling sharp objects. Wash hands immediately after coming in contact with copper(II) sulfate solution.*
2. Dip the nail in the $CuSO_4$ solution. (See Figure 3.) Predict what changes will happen to the appearance of the nail and the solution. After 5 min, pull the nail from the solution and place it on a paper towel. Record the colors of the nail and the solution in Table 1.
3. Put the nail back into the solution and observe further color changes.

Figure 2

Splint

Baking soda

Figure 3

Data and Observations

Part A—Two Reactants→One Product

1. Color of steel wool before burning:

_____

2. Prediction of changes in the heated steel wool:

_____

_____

Laboratory Activity 2 (continued)

3. Color of burned steel wool:

_____

Part B—One Reactant→Two Products

4. Prediction of changes in the heated baking soda:

_____

5. Description of deposits inside heated test tube:

_____

6. Observations of flaming splint:

_____

Part C—Two Reactants→Two Products

7. Prediction of changes in nail and $CuSO_4$ solution:

_____

Table 1

Observation time	Color of nail	Color of CuSO₄ solution
Before reaction	**8.**	**9.**
After reaction	**10.**	**11.**

Questions and Conclusions

1. Identify the two reactants in the heating of steel wool.

_____

_____

2. How does the heat from the flame affect the reactants when steel wool is heated?

_____

_____

3. What evidence suggests that at least two reactants were formed when $NaHCO_3$ was heated?

_____

_____

4. Was the heating of $NaHCO_3$ an endothermic or exothermic reaction? Explain your answer.

_____

_____

Laboratory Activity 2 (continued)

5. From your observations, does the reaction of an iron nail with the copper (II) sulfate yield more than one product?

_____

_____

_____

_____

6. Was the addition of the iron nail to the copper (II) sulfate solution an endothermic or exothermic reaction?

_____

_____

Strategy Check

_____ Can you identify the reactants and products of a chemical reaction?

_____ Can you write a word equation for a chemical reaction?

_____ Can you write a balanced chemical equation using chemical symbols?

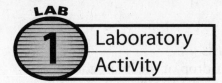

Acids, Bases, and Indicators

LAB 1 Laboratory Activity

You can express the acidity of a solution by using a pH scale. The pH of a solution is a measure of the concentration of the hydronium ions (H_3O^+) in that solution. The pH scale ranges in value from 0 to 14. Acids have pH values less than 7. Bases have pH values greater than 7. A neutral solution has a pH value of exactly 7.

The pH of a solution can be determined by using an indicator. An indicator is usually an organic compound that changes color at certain pH values. A universal indicator is a mixture of indicators that can be used to determine a wide range of pH values.

Strategy

You will investigate how a universal indicator is affected by acidic and basic solutions. You will determine the pH of several common liquids.

Materials

96-well microplate
sheet of white paper
plastic microtip pipette
distilled water

0.1M hydrochloric acid solution, HCl(*aq*)
0.01M sodium hydroxide solution, NaOH(*aq*)

universal indicator solution
samples of lemon juice, milk, and liquid soap

WARNING: *The sodium hydroxide and hydrochloric acid are corrosive. The universal indicator can cause stains. Avoid contacting these solutions with your skin or clothing. Wear an apron and goggles during this experiment.*

Procedure

Part A—Preparing a Color Scale

1. Place the 96-well microplate on a piece of white paper on a flat surface. Have the numbered columns of the microplate at the top and the lettered rows at the left.

2. Using the microtip pipette, add 9 drops of the distilled water to each of the wells A2–A11.

3. Use the pipette to add 10 drops of the hydrochloric acid solution to well A1. Rinse the pipette with distilled water.

4. Use the pipette to add 10 drops of the sodium hydroxide solution to well A12. Rinse the pipette with distilled water.

5. Use the pipette to transfer one drop of hydrochloric acid solution from well A1 to well A2. Return any solution remaining in the pipette to well A1, making sure the pipette is empty. Mix the contents of well A2 by drawing the solution into the pipette and then returning it to well A2.

6. Using the pipette, transfer one drop of the solution in well A2 to well A3. Return any solution remaining in the pipette to well A2.

Mix the contents of well A3 by drawing the solution into the pipette and then returning it to the well.

7. Repeat step 6, transferring A3 into A4, A4 into A5, and A5 into A6. Rinse the pipette with distilled water.

8. Use the pipette to transfer one drop of sodium hydroxide solution from well A12 to A11. Return any sodium hydroxide solution remaining in the pipette to well A12. Mix the contents of well A11 by drawing the solution into the pipette and then returning it to well A11.

9. Using the pipette, transfer one drop of the solution in well A11 to A10. Return any solution remaining in the pipette to well A11. Mix the contents of well A10 by drawing the solution into the pipette and then returning it to the well.

 SCI 5.e. Students know how to determine whether a solution is acidic, basic, or neutral.

Laboratory Activity 1 (continued)

10. Repeat step 9 for wells A10 and A9. Do not transfer solution from well A8 to well A7. Well A7 will contain only distilled water. Rinse the pipette with distilled water.

11. Use the pipette to add 1 drop of the universal indicator to each of the wells A1–A12. Rinse the pipette with distilled water.

12. Observe the solutions in each well. Record the color of the solution in each well in Table 1 in the Data and Observations section.

Part B—Determining the pH of Solutions

1. Use the pipette to place 9 drops of lemon juice in well C1. Rinse the pipette with distilled water.

2. Place 9 drops of milk in well C2 and 9 drops of liquid soap in well C3. Rinse the pipette in distilled water after each addition.

3. Using the pipette, add 1 drop of the universal indicator to each of the wells C1–C3.

4. Observe the solution in each well. Record the name of the solution and its color in Table 2.

Part C—Analysis

1. By adding 1 drop of the hydrochloric acid solution in well A1 to the 9 drops of water in well A2, the concentration of the hydrochloric acid in well A2 was reduced to 1/10 that of well A1. With each dilution in wells A1–A6, you reduced the concentration of the acid from one well to the next by 1/10. Likewise, by diluting the sodium hydroxide solution, the concentration of the sodium hydroxide solution is decreased by 1/10 from wells A12–A8. Because of these dilutions, the pH value of the solution in each of the wells A1–A12 will be the same as the number of the well, as shown in Figure 1. For example, the pH of the solution in well A3 will be 3.

2. The color of the solutions in wells A1–A12 can be used to determine the pH of other solutions that are tested with the universal indicator. You can determine the pH of a solution by comparing its color with the color of the solution in wells A1–A12. Using Table 1, determine the pH values of the solutions that you tested in Part B of the procedure. Record the pH values in Table 2.

Figure 1

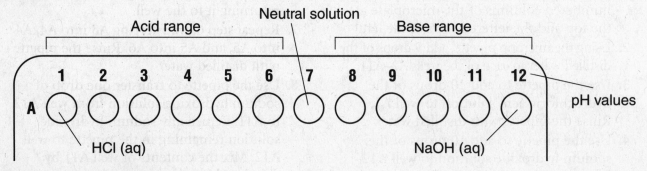

Data and Observations

Table 1

Well	A1	A2	A3	A4	A5	A6
Color						
Well	A7	A8	A9	A10	A11	A12
Color						

| Laboratory Activity 1 (continued) |

Table 2

Solution	Color	pH

Questions and Conclusions

1. What is the range of pH values of acids and bases?

_____

2. Classify the solutions that you tested in Part B as acids or bases.

_____

3. Distilled water is neutral. What is its pH value? What color will water appear if it is tested with the universal indicator solution?

_____

_____

4. What is a universal indicator?

_____

_____

Strategy Check

_____ Can you determine how acidic and basic solutions affect a universal indicator?

_____ Can you determine the pH of several common liquids?

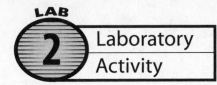

Acid Rain

LAB 2 Laboratory Activity

Have you ever seen stained buildings, crumbling statues, or trees that have lost their leaves because of acid rain? Acid rain is a harmful form of pollution. Its effects are also easy to see. Acid rain is precipitation that contains high concentrations of acids. The precipitation may be in the form of rain, snow, sleet, or fog.

The major products formed from burning fossil fuels such as coal and gasoline are carbon dioxide and water. However, nitrogen dioxide and sulfur dioxide are also formed. These gases dissolve in precipitation to form acid rain.

When acid rain falls on a pond or lake, the acidity of the water increases. The rise in the acidity is usually harmful to organisms living in the water. If the acidity becomes too high, all living things in the water will die. The pond or lake is then considered to be "dead."

Strategy

You will generate a gas that represents acid rain.
You will observe the reaction of this gas with water.
You will demonstrate how the gas can spread from one location to another.

> **SCI 5.e.** Students know how to determine whether a solution is acidic, basic, or neutral.

Equipment

96-well microplate	forceps	white paper
plastic microtip pipette	calcium carbonate, CaCO$_3$(cr)	hydrochloric acid solution,
distilled water	scissors	HCl(aq)
paper towel	soda straw	watch or clock
universal indicator solution	sealable, plastic sandwich bag	

WARNING: *The hydrochloric acid solution is corrosive. The universal indicator solution can cause stains. Avoid contacting these solutions with your skin or clothing. Wear an apron and goggles during this experiment.*

Procedure

1. Place the microplate on a flat surface.
2. Using the plastic microtip pipette, completely fill all the wells except A1, A12, D6, H1, and H12 with distilled water.
3. Use a paper towel to wipe away any water on the surface of the microplate.
4. Using the microtip pipette, add 1 drop of the indicator solution to each well containing water. Rinse the microtip pipette with distilled water.
5. Use the forceps to add a small lump of calcium carbonate to well D6.
6. Use the scissors to cut four 1-cm lengths of soda straw. Insert one length of soda straw in each of the wells A1, A12, H1, and H12 as shown in Figure 1. Cut a 0.5-cm length of soda straw and place it in well D6.
7. Carefully place the microplate into the plastic sandwich bag and seal the bag. Place the bag on the piece of white paper.
8. Using the scissors, punch a small hole in the plastic bag directly over well D6.
9. Fill the microtip pipette one-fourth full with the hydrochloric acid solution.
10. Slip the tip of the pipette through the hole above well D6. Direct the stem of the pipette into the soda straw in well D6.
11. Add 4 drops of hydrochloric acid to the well. Observe the surrounding wells.
12. After 30 seconds, note any color changes in the surrounding wells. Record a color change in the solution in a well by marking a positive sign (+) in the corresponding well of the microplate shown in Figure 2a in Data and Observations.
13. Repeat steps 11 and 12 two more times. Record your two sets of observations in Figure 2b and Figure 2c, respectively.

Laboratory Activity 2 (continued)

Figure 1

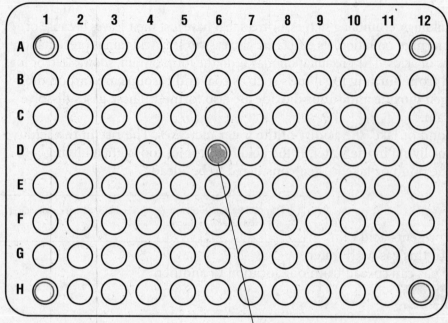

Calcium carbonate

Data and Observations

Figure 2a

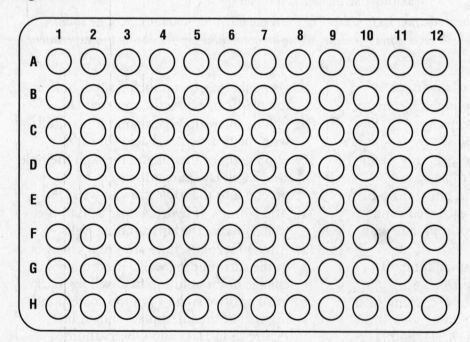

Laboratory Activity 2 (continued)

Figure 2b

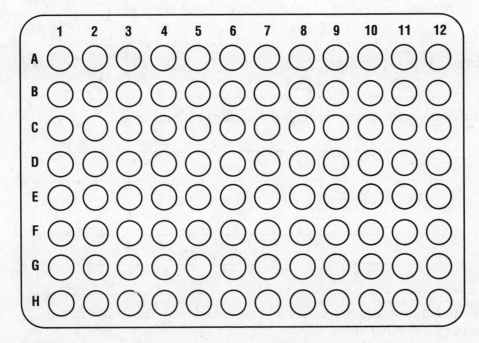

Figure 2c

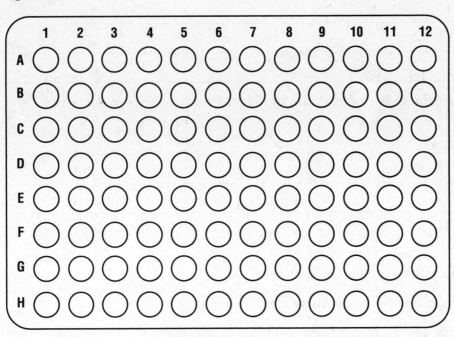

Laboratory Activity 2 (continued)

Questions and Conclusions

1. Calcium carbonate and hydrochloric acid react to produce a gas. What is the gas?

_____

2. What does this gas represent in this experiment?

_____

3. What physical process caused the gas to move through the air in the plastic bag?

_____

_____

4. Why were the lengths of soda straws placed in wells A1, A12, H1, and H12?

_____

_____

_____

5. Discuss how this experiment demonstrates how acid rain can spread from the source of the chemicals that produce acid rain to other areas.

_____

_____

_____

6. What factors that may cause the spread of acid rain in the environment are not demonstrated in this model experiment?

_____

_____

_____

Strategy Check

_____ Can you generate a gas that represents acid rain?

_____ Can you detect the reaction of this gas with water?

_____ Can you show how the gas can spread from one place to another?

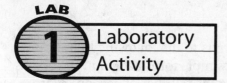

Carbohydrates: Chemistry and Identification

Carbohydrates make up a large group of chemical compounds found in cells. Carbohydrates are an energy source or are used in making cell structures. There are three different groups of carbohydrates. They are called monosaccharides, disaccharides, and polysaccharides. *Saccharide* means sugar.

Strategy

You will write simple formulas for several carbohydrates.
You will read structural formulas for several carbohydrates.
You will use models to construct the three main types of carbohydrates.
You will identify the three main types of carbohydrates by using chemical tests.
You will test different food samples to determine what type of carbohydrate they contain.

Materials

beaker (pyrex)
droppers
glass marking pencil or labels
hot plate
test tubes
test-tube holder

apple juice
Benedict's solution
disaccharide solution
honey solution
iodine solution
monosaccharide solution

oat solution
polysaccharide solution
powdered sugar solution
table sugar solution
gloves

WARNING: *Do not taste, eat, or drink any materials used in the lab. Inform your teacher if you come in contact with any chemicals.*

Procedure

Part A—Carbohydrate Models

1. A single molecule sugar is called a mono-saccharide. The prefix *mono-* means one. Glucose and fructose are monosaccharides.

Examine the structural formulas of these sugars in Figure 1. What three chemical elements are present in the monosaccharides?

Figure 1

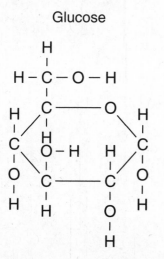

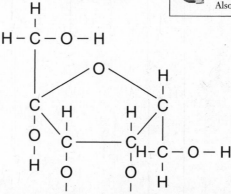

SCI 6.b. Students know that living organisms are made of molecules consisting largely of carbon, hydrogen, nitrogen, oxygen, phosphorus, and sulfur. Also covers **SCI 6.c.**

Laboratory Activity 1 (continued)

2. Add subscripts to the following to indicate the correct simple formula. Fill in the blanks by counting the total number of carbon, hydrogen, and oxygen atoms in each molecule.

   a. glucose C__ H__ O__

   b. fructose C__ H__ O__

3. Are there two times as many hydrogen atoms as oxygen atoms in a molecule of

   a. glucose? _____

   b. fructose? _____

Two monosaccharide sugar molecules can join chemically to form a larger carbohydrate molecule called a double sugar, or disaccharide. The prefix *di-* means two. By chemically joining a glucose with a fructose molecule, a double sugar called sucrose is produced as modeled in Figure 2.

4. Add subscripts to the following to indicate the correct simple formula. Fill in the blanks by counting the number of carbon, hydrogen, and oxygen atoms in each molecule.

   sucrose C__ H__ O__

5. Are there two times as many hydrogen atoms as oxygen atoms in a disaccharide?

   _____

6. How many monosaccharide molecules are needed to form one sucrose molecule?

   _____

Figure 2

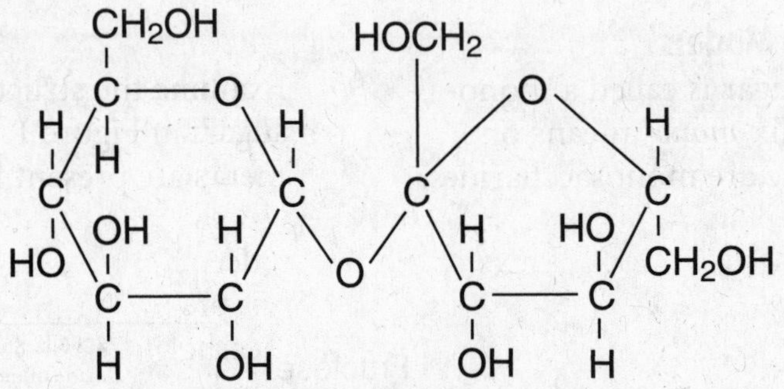

Sucrose

Laboratory Activity 1 (continued)

Part B—Identification of Carbohydrates

Just as double sugars were formed from two single sugar molecules, polysaccharides are formed when many single sugars are joined. The prefix *poly*– means many. Starch, glycogen, and cellulose are the three most common polysaccharides. They consist of long chains of glucose molecules joined together.

Chemical Tests on Known Carbohydrates
Benedict's Test

1. Pour water into a 500-mL beaker until it is half full. Bring the water to a boil on a hot plate. **WARNING:** *Do not touch hot plate. Water is very hot. Use care when handling hot liquids.* The boiling water is called a hot water bath.

2. Number three clean test tubes 1 to 3. Using Figure 3 as a guide, with a clean dropper for each tube, add the following:
   Tube 1—30 drops of monosaccharide solution
   Tube 2—30 drops of disaccharide solution
   Tube 3—30 drops of polysaccharide solution

3. Add 30 drops of Benedict's solution to each tube. **WARNING:** *If you spill Benedict's solution, rinse with water and call your teacher.*

4. Place the three test tubes into the hot water bath for 5 min.

5. Use a test-tube holder to remove the tubes from the hot water bath. **WARNING:** *Water and test tubes are very hot. Handle test tubes only with a test-tube holder.*

6. Observe any color changes in the solutions. NOTE: A color change may or may not occur when Benedict's solution is added to a carbohydrate and then heated. A change from blue to green, yellow, orange, or red occurs if a monosaccharide is present. The blue color will remain after heating if a disaccharide or polysaccharide is present.

7. Record the colors of the solutions in the test tubes in column three of Table 1.

8. Number three clean test tubes 1 to 3. Using Figure 4 as a guide, with a clean dropper for each tube, add the following:
   Tube 1—30 drops of monosaccharide solution
   Tube 2—30 drops of disaccharide solution
   Tube 3—30 drops of polysaccharide solution

9. Add 4 drops of iodine solution to each tube. **WARNING:** *Iodine is poisonous. Do not allow iodine to get on your hands. Wash immediately if iodine comes in contact with your skin. Do not inhale iodine fumes.*

10. Mix the contents of each tube by gently swirling.

11. Record in column four of Table 1 the color of the solutions in the three tubes. NOTES: A color change may or may not occur when iodine solution is added to a carbohydrate. A change from its original rust color to deep blue-black occurs if a polysaccharide is present. The original color of the carbohydrate remains if a disaccharide or monosaccharide sugar is present.

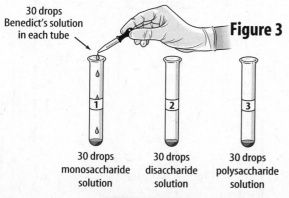

30 drops Benedict's solution in each tube

Figure 3

30 drops monosaccharide solution

30 drops disaccharide solution

30 drops polysaccharide solution

BENEDICT'S TEST

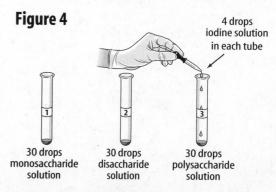

Figure 4

4 drops iodine solution in each tube

30 drops monosaccharide solution

30 drops disaccharide solution

30 drops polysaccharide solution

IODINE TEST

Laboratory Activity 1 (continued)

Chemical Tests on Unknown Carbohydrates

You have tested known carbohydrates, so you are now ready to test some unknown substances. By comparing results of the Benedict's and iodine tests in Table 1, you should be able to classify monosaccharides, disaccharides, or polysaccharides.

12. Number five clean test tubes 1 to 5. Using Figure 5 as a guide, with a clean dropper for each tube, add the following:
    Tube 1—20 drops of honey
    Tube 2—20 drops of liquid oats
    Tube 3—20 drops of table sugar solution
    Tube 4—20 drops of apple juice
    Tube 5—20 drops of powdered sugar solution

13. Add 30 drops of Benedict's solution to each test tube.

14. Place all five test tubes into a hot water bath for 5 min.

15. Remove the test tubes from the bath with a test-tube holder and note any color changes. Record the color of the solutions in Table 2.

16. Using Figure 6 as a guide, prepare five more test tubes containing the same substances just used (honey, oats, and so on). Do not add Benedict's solution.

17. Add 4 drops of iodine solution to each tube and mix by swirling.

18. Observe any color changes and record them in Table 2.

19. On the basis of your results, classify each carbohydrate as a monosaccharide, disaccharide, or polysaccharide. Record your answers in Table 2.

Figure 5

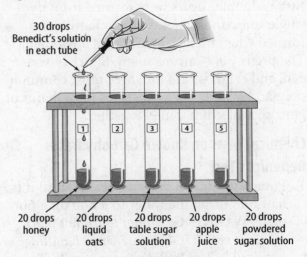

30 drops
Benedict's solution
in each tube

20 drops honey | 20 drops liquid oats | 20 drops table sugar solution | 20 drops apple juice | 20 drops powdered sugar solution

BENEDICT'S TEST

Figure 6

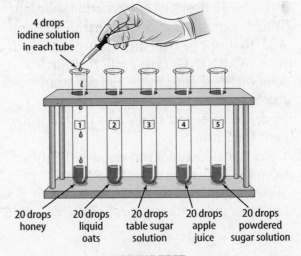

4 drops
iodine solution
in each tube

20 drops honey | 20 drops liquid oats | 20 drops table sugar solution | 20 drops apple juice | 20 drops powdered sugar solution

IODINE TEST

| Laboratory Activity 1 (continued) |

Data and Observations

Table 1

Tube number	Carbohydrate type	Change in color after heating with Benedict's	Change in color after adding iodine
1	Monosaccharide		
2	Disaccharide		
3	Polysaccharide		

Table 2

Carbohydrate	Benedict's color	Iodine color	Carbohydrate type
Honey			
Oats			
Table sugar			
Apple juice			
Powdered sugar			

Questions and Conclusions

1. Name the three categories of carbohydrates studied in this investigation.

   _____

2. What three elements are present in all carbohydrates?

   _____

3. Give two examples of each of the following sugars.
   a. monosaccharides

   _____

   b. disaccharides

   _____

   c. polysaccharides

   _____

Laboratory Activity 1 (continued)

4. **a.** How many times larger is the number of hydrogen atoms than oxygen atoms in all

   carbohydrates? _____

   b. In water? _____

5. *Mono-* means one, *di-* means two, and *poly-* means many. Why are these terms used in describing the three types of sugars?

   _____

6. How can you tell by using Benedict's and iodine solutions if a sugar is a
   a. monosaccharide?

   _____

   b. disaccharides?

   _____

   c. polysaccharides?

   _____

7. A certain sugar has no change in color when tested with Benedict's solution. Can you tell what type of saccharide it is? Explain.

   _____

   _____

8. A certain sugar has a color change in Benedict's solution. Can you tell what type of saccharide it is? Explain.

   _____

   _____

9. Give an example of a food for each of the following sugars.

   a. monosaccharide _____

   b. disaccharides _____

   c. polysaccharides _____

Strategy Check

_____ Can you write simple formulas for some carbohydrates?

_____ Can you read and understand structural formulas for carbohydrates?

_____ Can you make models of the three main types of carbohydrates?

_____ Can you identify monosaccharides, disaccharides, and polysaccharides by means of chemical tests?

_____ Can you test food samples to determine whether they contain carbohydrates and what kind they contain?

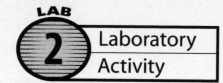

Proteins: Chemistry and Identification

Living things are made up of many different molecules. One important group of chemical molecules is proteins. Proteins make up the bulk of all solid material within your body and the bodies of other animals. Your muscle, skin, hair, and inside organs are largely protein. Proteins are essential for body growth and repair. They also make up some hormones that are involved in the chemical control of the body.

Strategy

You will recognize simple formulas for amino acids.
You will use models of different amino acids to construct a protein molecule.
You will use chemical tests to determine if a protein is present in a substance.

Materials

dropper	test tubes	dog hair (white)
glass-making pencil or labels	test-tube rack (or tin can)	egg white (hard-boiled)
paper models	absorbent cotton	fingernail clippings
scissors	cream cheese	nitric acid 3.0M

Procedure

Part A—Models of Protein: Amino Acids, Building Blocks of Protein

Proteins are complex molecules made up of smaller molecules called amino acids. There are many different amino acids found in nature. The element nitrogen (N) is present in all amino acids.

1. Examine the structural formulas of the four representative amino acids shown in Figure 1, and name the four elements present in these amino acids.

_____

_____

2. What is the simple formula for the following amino acids
   a. glycine

   C_____H_____O_____N_____

   b. alanine

   C_____H_____O_____N_____

   c. valine

   C_____H_____O_____N_____

   d. threonine

   C_____H_____O_____N_____

SCI 6.b. Students know that living organisms are made of molecules consisting largely of carbon, hydrogen, nitrogen, oxygen, phosphorus, and sulfur. Also covers SCI 6.c.

Figure 1

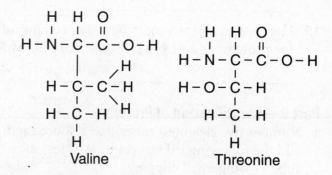

Laboratory Activity 2 (continued)

3. How do the simple formulas for all of the amino acids differ?

_____

4. Note the upper right corner of each amino acid. These ends have a special arrangement of carbon, oxygen, and hydrogen atoms. This end arrangement is called a carboxyl group. Circle the carboxyl group on each structural formula in Figure 1.

5. Note the upper left corner of each amino acid. These ends have a special arrangement of nitrogen and hydrogen atoms. The end arrangement is called an amino group. Use dashed lines to circle the amino groups on the structural formulas in Figure 1.

6. How does the number of hydrogen atoms compare with the number of oxygen atoms in each amino acid?

_____

7. Several amino acids must be joined in a chain to form a protein molecule. You can show how amino acids join by using models. Use the paper models given to you by your teacher to complete this section.

8. Cut out the four amino acid models. **WARNING:** *Always be extremely careful with scissors. Cut along the solid lines only.* Attempt to join the amino acids.

9. Join the molecules by removing as many —OH groups and —H groups as needed from the amino acids. All four amino acids can be joined in this manner to form a protein. Join them in the order valine—threonine—alanine—glycine.

10. Join the leftover —OH and —H ends.

11. What chemical substance is formed with the —OHs and —Hs joined?

_____

12. How many molecules of water are formed when four amino acids are joined?

_____

13. What chemical compound is formed when the four amino acids are joined?

_____

14. Describe the difference between an amino acid molecule and a protein molecule.

_____

15. Use your models to construct two proteins different from the one you already made. Identify the proteins as *a* or *b* and list the order in which you connected the amino acids.

_____

Part B—Identification of Proteins

1. Number five clean test tubes 1 to 5. Place them in a test-tube rack. Using Figure 2 as a guide, add the following substances to each test tube:

tube 1—fingernail clippings

tube 2—egg white, hard-boiled

tube 3—absorbent cotton

tube 4—dog hair, white

tube 5—cream cheese

Lab Activities

Laboratory Activity 2 (continued)

2. Add 5 drops of nitric acid to each test tube. **WARNING:** *Nitric acid is harmful to skin and clothing. Rinse with water if spillage occurs. Call your teacher.*

3. A substance containing protein will turn yellow when nitric acid is added to it. No color change to yellow indicates that the substance being tested has no protein. Wait several minutes. Then record the color of the items placed in each tube in Table 1.

4. On the basis of the nitric acid test, indicate in the last column of Table 1 if the substances tested contain protein.

Figure 2

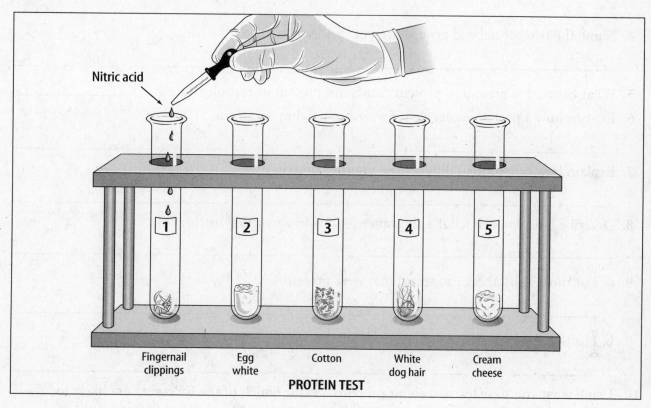

Nitric acid

1 2 3 4 5

Fingernail clippings | Egg white | Cotton | White dog hair | Cream cheese

PROTEIN TEST

Data and Observations

Table 1

Substance	Color change due to nitric acid	Substance tested is a protein (answer yes or no)
1. Fingernail		
2. Egg white		
3. Cotton		
4. Dog hair		
5. Cream cheese		

Laboratory Activity 2 (continued)

Questions and Conclusions

1. Name four amino acids. _____

2. How are amino acids used by living things? _____

_____

3. List several of your body parts that are protein. _____

_____

4. Name the two special end groups present in amino acids.

_____

5. What element is present in protein that is not present in carbohydrates? _____

6. Explain how a protein molecule is formed in a living organism.

_____

7. Explain how one protein differs from another protein.

_____

8. Describe how you can tell if a substance is a protein by using nitric acid.

_____

9. a. List those substances you tested that were protein.

_____

   b. List those substances you tested that were not protein.

_____

10. Using what you have learned about proteins, decide which of the following are likely to contain protein. Place a check mark on the line next to each substance that is a protein.

   a. bear claw _____   e. boiled egg _____

   b. chicken _____   f. human hair _____

   c. peanut oil _____   g. cheese cake _____

   d. maple syrup _____   h. 207 amino acids joined _____

Strategy Check

_____ Can you identify an amino acid from its formula?

_____ Can you construct a protein molecule using models of amino acids?

_____ Can you explain a test used to determine whether a substance contains a protein?

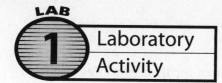

The Behavior of Comets

LAB 1 Laboratory Activity

One way scientists study the behavior and composition of comets is by observing them as they orbit the Sun. Observations made through telescopes and pictures sent back by space probes have led scientists to believe a comet is a mixture of ice and rock. Heat from the Sun vaporizes some of the comet's ice, which releases bits of rock and dust that form a cloud around the comet. Solar winds blowing on the cloud create the comet's tail. The intensity of the solar wind makes the tail point away from the Sun, no matter which direction the comet is facing. Because the comet is vaporizing when it becomes visible from Earth, each time we see a comet, we are witnessing its deterioration.

Strategy

You will model and observe the behavior of comets orbiting the Sun.
You will describe the behavior and draw inferences about the life of a
comet based on your observations.

Materials

newspaper
small electric fan
books or boxes
waxed paper
ruler

red, green, or blue construction paper (the
color should make water drops easy to see)
sand (not dirt)
ice (crushed, not in cubes)

SCI 4.e. Students know the appearance, general composition, relative position and size, and motion of objects in the solar system, including planets, planetary satellites, comets, and asteroids. Also covers **SCI 2.g.**

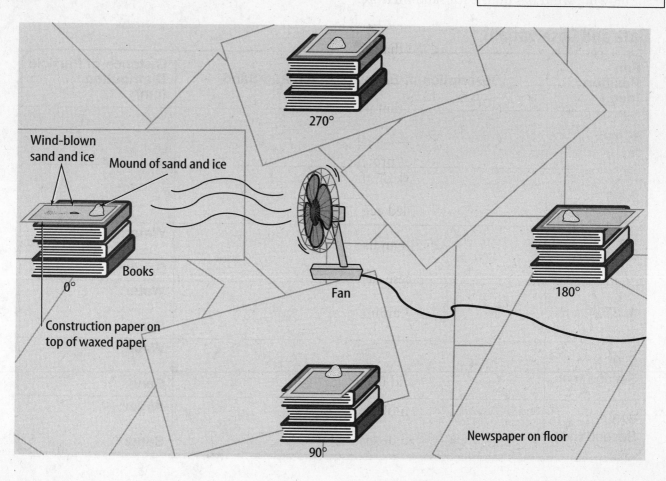

Wind-blown sand and ice

Mound of sand and ice

270°

Books

0°

Construction paper on top of waxed paper

Fan

90°

180°

Newspaper on floor

Laboratory Activity 1 (continued)

Procedure

1. Working in groups of four students, place newspaper on your lab table or the floor near an electric outlet. Put the fan in the middle of the newspaper. Place books or boxes at four positions around the fan. The first position should be 0° The next are at 90°, 180°, and 270°. Be sure to cover books with wax paper to protect them against any water spills.

2. Take a piece of colored construction paper about 23 cm × 15 cm and place it with its longer edge away from the fan. Do this for each position. See Figure 1. Then get a small mixture (about a tablespoon) of sand and ice and mound it on the paper at the end nearest the fan. Draw a line on the page around the mound of sand and ice.

3. Have one student carefully turn on the fan at the 0° position and observe the effect the blowing wind has on the ice/sand mixture.

Let the fan run for three minutes and then turn it off. Record your observation in the table provided.

4. Turn the fan so that it is pointing to the 90° position and repeat the procedure. Continue until the fan has run on all four positions and then repeat for position 0°. Turn the fan to the 90° position. Carefully turn on the fan one more time. Be sure to record all your observations in the table.

5. When you are finished, take your paper and carefully place it on the ground or tabletop. Try not to move any of the particles as you move the paper. Take your ruler and measure the distance the water drops and sand moved from their original position at the front of the paper. Record these distances in the last column of the table.

Data and Observations

Fan Position (deg.)	Description of Behavior of Ice and Sand	Distance of Particle Distribution (cm)
1. 0°		
2. 90°		
3. 180°		Water: Sand:
4. 270°		Water: Sand:
5. 0° Second trial		Water: Sand:
6. 90° Second trial		Water: Sand:

Laboratory Activity 1 (continued)

Questions and Conclusions

1. What is one behavior of the ice and sand you observed?

_____

_____

_____

2. How would you explain what you saw?

_____

_____

_____

3. How does this behavior demonstrate the similarities between your experiment and what we observe in a comet orbiting the Sun?

_____

_____

_____

4. Where does the water and dust from a melting comet go?

_____

_____

5. Using your answer from question 4, would you expect a comet to always die out? Explain your answer.

_____

_____

_____

Strategy Check

_____ Can you model the behavior of a comet orbiting the Sun?

_____ Can you describe this behavior based on what you know about the composition of comets?

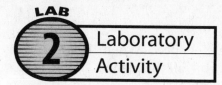

LAB 2 Laboratory Activity

Modeling the Orbits of Planets

The solar system is made up of the nine planets and other objects, like asteroids, which orbit the Sun. Do the nine planets take the same amount of time to complete their orbits? Do this activity to find out.

Strategy

You will model the solar system using students to represent planets.
You will model the orbits of planets.
You will plot the positions of planets on a chart.
You will predict future locations of planets.

SCI 4.e. Students know the appearance, general composition, relative position and size, and motion of objects in the solar system, including planets, planetary satellites, comets, and asteroids.

Materials

a large, clear area (40 m square)
a piece of string 25 m long (the string should be marked at each meter)
masking tape

Procedure

1. Working as a group, use the string and masking tape to mark out a circle 1 m across in an open area. Think of this circle as a bull's-eye. As Figure 1 shows, you'll mark out eight circles around this center circle. Make these other circles 3 m, 5 m, 7 m, 10 m, 12 m, 14 m, 16 m, and 18 m across.

2. Label each circle with the name of a planet. The innermost circle is Mercury, followed by Venus, Earth, Mars, Jupiter, Saturn, Uranus, Neptune, and Pluto. The circles represent the orbits of the planets.

3. Have one student stand in the middle of the innermost circle, holding the string. Have another student, holding the other end of the string, stand just beyond the outermost circle. Stretch the string tight and mark a straight line from the center of the innermost circle to beyond the outermost circle. This line is your reference line. It will help you to plot the planets' orbits.

Figure 1

Laboratory Activity 2 (continued)

4. Choose nine students in your group to represent the solar system's nine planets. Have them stand on the circle that represents their planet's orbit. They should stand at the place where the reference line crosses their planet's orbit.

5. When your teacher gives the signal, the "planets" should begin their orbits, moving in a clockwise direction at approximately

the same rate of speed. When "Earth" completes one orbit, all the planets should stop and stand in place.

6. Plot the location of the planets on the chart labeled Year 1 of Figure 2 in the Data and Observations section.

7. Repeat steps 5 and 6 three times. Use three different charts in Figure 2. Label the charts Year 2, Year 3, and Year 4.

Data and Observations

Figure 2

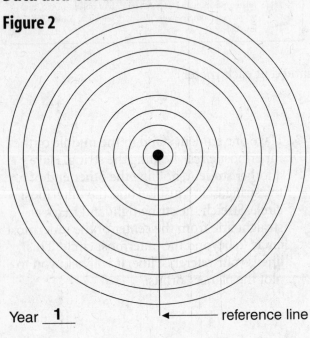

Year __1__ ← reference line

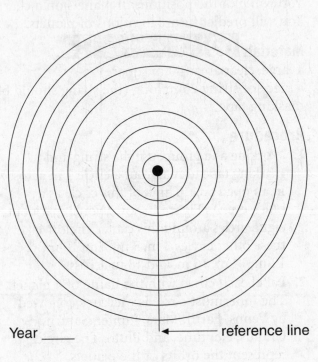

Year ____ ← reference line

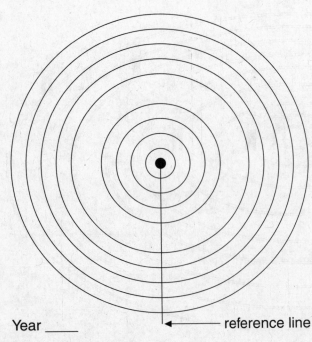

Year ____ ← reference line

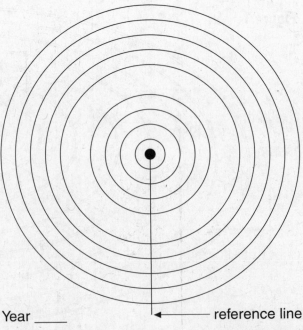

Year ____ ← reference line

Laboratory Activity 2 (continued)

Questions and Conclusions

1. The orbital period of a planet is the time it takes to complete one orbit. Which planet has the shortest orbital period?

   _____

2. Which planet has the longest orbital period?

   _____

3. In the time it took for the student representing Mars to orbit once, how many times did the student representing Earth orbit?

   _____

   _____

4. Imagine that you are about to launch a space probe to Jupiter and the planets are lined up as they were in the beginning of this activity. It will take five years for your probe to reach Jupiter.

   On Figure 3, mark the location of Jupiter in five years. Draw a line representing the path of your space probe.

Figure 3

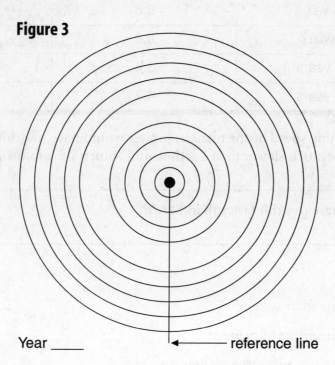

Year _____   ◄—— reference line

Laboratory Activity 2 (continued)

In this activity, the "planets" orbited at the same speed. In reality, planets orbit at different speeds. Also, the distances between the planets in the model did not accurately represent the true distances between the planets in the solar system. Table 1 shows the planets' actual orbital speeds and the distances between planets. Use the table to answer the questions that follow it.

Table 1

Planet	Orbital Period	Orbital speed (km/s)	Distance from sun (millions of km)
Mercury	88 days	47.9	58
Venus	225 days	35.0	108
Earth	1 year	29.8	150
Mars	1.88 years	24.1	228
Jupiter	11.86 years	13.1	778
Saturn	29.4 years	9.6	1,426
Uranus	84 years	6.8	2,871
Neptune	165 years	5.4	4,497
Pluto	249 years	4.7	5,914

5. To model the true orbiting speed of the planets, Jupiter would have to orbit almost 12 times slower than Earth. How much slower than Earth would Saturn have to orbit?

_____

6. Which planets would have to orbit faster than Earth?

_____

Strategy Check

_____ Can you model the solar system?

_____ Can you model the orbits of planets?

_____ Can you plot the positions of the planets on a chart?

_____ Can you predict future locations of planets?

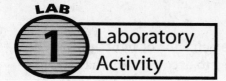

Absolute and Apparent Magnitudes

The apparent magnitude of a star, or how much light is received on Earth, can be confusing to an astronomer trying to measure the distance a star is from Earth. Apparent magnitude is much different from the absolute magnitude, which is the true measure of how much light the star emits. These two variables control the brightness of the stars we see in our night sky. The absolute magnitude is not the same for every star. It is determined by the amount of light it gives off. The second variable is the amount of light received on Earth. The mixing of these two variables can lead to misunderstanding about the size and distance of a star. That is why it is important to understand the characteristics of stars and light to be able to correctly determine what we see in the night sky.

Strategy

You will observe how light behaves over distance.

You will predict how two stars that are different in size and far away from each other may appear in the night sky.

 SCI 4.d. Students know that stars are the source of light for all bright objects in outer space and that the Moon and planets shine by reflected sunlight, not by their own light. Also covers **SCI 4.b.**

Materials

black construction paper
scissors
small flashlight

rubber bands
medium-sized nail
tape

measuring tape or meterstick
white correction fluid
*chalk
* markers
* Alternate materials

Procedure

1. Students will work in groups of three to four. Use your scissors to cut a piece of black construction paper large enough to comfortably cover the light end of the flashlight.

2. Cover the end of the flashlight with the paper and secure it in place with a rubber band. Take the sharp end of the nail and carefully poke a single hole in the center of the paper covering. The smaller the hole the better.

3. Find a wall or hard surface on which you can tape a background of more black construction paper. An area about one meter square would be best for the experiment. An alternate choice would be to use the black- or white-board in the classroom. If you do use a wall, write only with the appropriate materials, such as chalk or erasable marker.

4. At a distance of two meters or six feet from the wall, mark a spot with tape on the ground. Then mark the next interval at 1.3 meters or four feet. The last mark is at 0.6 meters or two feet.

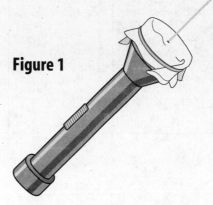

Figure 1

5. Ask your instructor to darken the room as much as possible. One student will stand at the six foot mark and turn on the flashlight. The other students will mark the edges of the diameter of the circle of light made by the flashlight with correction fluid, chalk, or markers. Be sure to notice the intensity of the inner and outer regions of the circle of light. You will record this in the data table provided.

Laboratory Activity 1 (continued)

6. Repeat this procedure at the closer interval. Then repeat one more time at the closest interval. Look at the intensity of the light instead. When is it most intense and where is it very diffuse? Record these observations in your table.

7. Observe the behavior of light at different intervals. Try to account for what you observe by what you know. For instance, you know the amount of light exiting the flashlight has not changed at all during the experiment. So what is happening to the dispersal of light? Record your hypothesis in the space marked "Hypothesis for the dispersal of light."

Data and Observations

Table 1

Diameter of Light Circle (cm)			Observations about Intensity of Light (cm)
Trial 1	Trial 2	Trial 3	

Laboratory Activity 1 (continued)

According to your experiment, your circle of light changed in size as you got closer to the wall. The intensity, or brightness, also changed. How would you account for this? Write your hypothesis in the space below.

Hypothesis for the dispersal of light: _____

_____

_____

_____

Questions and Conclusions

1. The circle of light produced by your flashlight on the wall was larger when you were farther away from the wall. Was the light more or less intense? How do you account for this?

_____

_____

_____

2. The circle of light got smaller as you approached the wall. Was the light more or less intense? How do you account for this?

_____

_____

_____

_____

3. As a result of your experiment, would you expect a star to appear brighter when closer to or farther from the Earth? Explain your answer.

_____

_____

_____

4. If you used a bigger and brighter flashlight and repeated the same experiment, what would you expect your results to be like? Explain your answer.

_____

_____

_____

_____

Laboratory Activity 1 (continued)

5. Suppose you were going to perform the experiment with two students: One holds a weak flashlight; the other a strong flashlight. How would you place the students so that the circles of light on the wall were exactly the same size? Explain your answer in terms of magnitude.

_____

_____

_____

_____

6. How would you model the difference in absolute magnitude between the two flashlights?

_____

_____

_____

_____

7. Predict what an astronomer would look for if he or she wanted to determine the size and heat of a star and its distance from the Earth. Would it be a good idea to watch the star over a long period?

_____

_____

_____

_____

Strategy Check

_____ Can you observe how light behaves over distance?

_____ Can you predict how two stars that are different in size and far away from each other may appear in the night sky?

Spectral Analysis

The photograph of the spectrum of a star, sorted by color across a plate, will reveal spectral lines upon close examination. The lines are produced by elements in a star at high temperature. These lines represent the chemical composition of the star. Each element has its own "fingerprint." To analyze the spectra of stars, scientists collected spectra of all the known elements. If we compare the spectral lines of an unknown star with the spectral lines of elements, we can determine the chemical composition of the star. More recently, we have discovered not only the composition of the stars but also their temperatures, their rotational rate, and their relative motion with regard to Earth.

Strategy

You will construct a simple spectral analyzer.
You will determine the composition of a star using the spectral analyzer.
You will determine other characteristics of a star by comparing the spectral lines with a standard.

Materials

scissors

Procedure

1. Turn to the third page of this lab. Cut out the pull tab card; the spectroscope fingerprints card; and Stars B, C, and D along the dashed lines.

2. Make five slits along the dashed lines A, B, C, D, and E on the fingerprints card.

3. From left to right, insert "Pull Tab Out" up through slit E, down through slit D, up through slit C, down through slit B, and up through slit A.

4. Compare the lines of each known element with the lines of Star A. If lines match, then that element is present in Star A. Record your findings in Table 1.

5. Star B, Star C, and Star D are provided for further study and comparison. Each can be placed over Star A.

Data and Observations

Table 1

Star	Chemical Composition	Other Characteristics
A		
B		
C		
D		

SCI 4.b. Students know that the Sun is one of many stars in the Milky Way galaxy and that stars may differ in size, temperature, and color. Also covers **SCI 4.d.**

Laboratory Activity 2 (continued)

Questions and Conclusions

1. When you hear someone say that neon lights look beautiful, what color comes to mind? What color is suggested by the "fingerprints" of neon?

_____

_____

_____

_____

2. Did any of the stars have the same chemical composition? Look at the table.

_____

_____

_____

3. Sometimes scientists see spectral lines that do not fit the usual pattern. The lines might be shifted from their usual positions. This may suggest that the star is moving either toward the observer (shift toward the blue) or away from the observer (shift toward the red). Look at the spectral lines for Star B and Star D. Star B is the standard for comparison. How is Star D different? What is a possible explanation for the difference?

_____

_____

_____

_____

4. If the scientist sees the spectral lines wider than usual, he or she relates this spectral broadening to either rotational speed (the broader the faster), temperature (the broader the hotter), or pressure (the broader the greater pressure). Look at the spectral lines for Star B and Star C. Star B is the standard. How is Star C different? What could be a possible explanation?

_____

_____

_____

_____

Strategy Check

_____ Can you construct a simple spectral analyzer?

_____ Can you determine the composition of a star using the spectral analyzer?

_____ Can you determine other characteristics of a star by comparing the spectral lines with a standard?

Laboratory Activity 2 (continued)

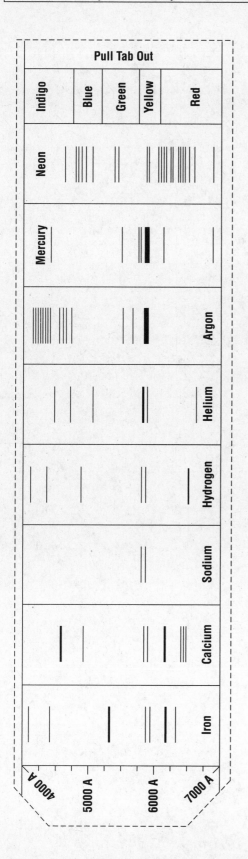

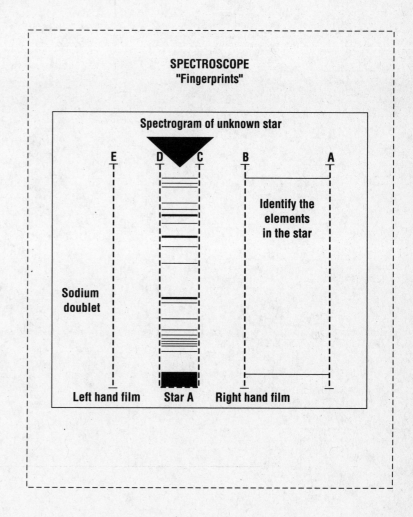

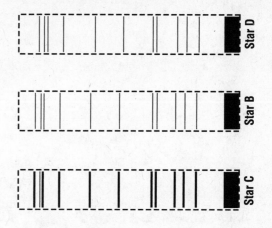

Inquiry Activities

Acids and Bases

SCI 5.e. Students know how to determine whether a solution is acidic, basic, or neutral.

You can express the acidity of a solution by using a pH scale. The pH of a solution is a measure of the concentration of the hydronium ions in that solution. The pH scale ranges in value from 0 to 14. Acids have pH values less than 7. Bases have pH values greater than 7. A neutral solution has a pH value of 7.0. The pH of a solution can be determined by using an indicator. An indicator is usually an organic compound that changes color at a certain pH value. A universal indicator is a mixture of indicators that can be used to determine a wide range of pH values.

Materials
- 96-well microplate
- plastic microtip pipette
- sheet of white paper
- distilled water
- hydrochloric acid solution, HCl(*aq*)
- sodium hydroxide solution, NaOH(*aq*)
- universal indicator solution
- samples of lemon juice, milk, liquid soap, ammonia, vinegar, baking soda, colorless soda, baking powder, antacid, tap water, and salt water

What You'll Investigate
In this experiment, you will investigate how a universal indicator is affected by acidic and basic solutions and determine the pH of several common liquids.

Procedure
WARNING: *The sodium hydroxide and hydrochloric acid solutions are corrosive. The universal indicator can cause stains. Do not allow these solutions to contact your skin or clothing.*

Part 1—Preparing a Color Scale
1. Wear an apron and goggles.
2. Place the 96-well microplate on a piece of white paper on a flat surface. Place the numbered columns of the microplate at the top and the lettered rows at the left.
3. Using the microtip pipette, add 9 drops of distilled water to wells A2–A11.
4. Use the pipette to add 10 drops of the hydrochloric acid solution to well A1. Rinse the pipette with distilled water.
5. Use the pipette to add 10 drops of the sodium hydroxide solution to well A12. Rinse the pipette with distilled water.

6. Use the pipette to transfer 1 drop of hydrochloric acid solution from well A1 to well A2. Return any solution remaining in the pipette to well A1, making sure the pipette is empty. Mix the contents of well A2 by drawing the solution into the pipette and then returning it to well A2.
7. Using the pipette, transfer 1 drop of the solution in well A2 to well A3. Return any remaining in the pipette to well A2. Mix the contents of well A3 by drawing the solution into the pipette and returning it to the well.
8. Repeat step 7 for wells A3, A4, and A5. Rinse the pipette with distilled water.
9. Use the pipette to transfer 1 drop of sodium hydroxide solution from well A12 to A11. Return any remaining in the pipette to well A12. Mix the contents of well A11 by drawing the solution into the pipette and returning it to well A11.

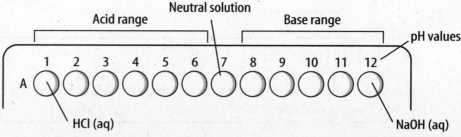

10. Using the pipette, transfer 1 drop of the solution in well A11 to A10. Return any solution remaining in the pipette to well A11. Mix the contents of well A10 by drawing the solution into the pipette and then returning it to the well.

11. Repeat step 10 for wells A10 and A9. Do not transfer solution from well A8 to well A7. Well A7 will contain only distilled water. Rinse the pipette with distilled water.

12. Use the pipette to add 1 drop of the universal indicator to each of the wells A1–A12. Rinse the pipette with distilled water.

13. Observe the solutions in each well. Record the color of each in **Table 1**.

Data and Observations
Part 1—Preparing a Color Scale

Table 1

Well	1	2	3	4	5	6
Color						
Well	7	8	9	10	11	12
Color						

Conclude and Apply

1. What are the pH values of acids and of bases?

_____

2. Classify the solutions that you tested in Part 2 as acids or bases.

_____

3. Distilled water is neutral. What is its pH value? What color will water appear if it is tested with the universal indicator solution?

_____

4. What is a universal indicator?

_____

Part 2—Determining the pH of Solutions

1. Choose four of the solutions from the list. Decide on two you believe are acidic and two you believe are basic.

2. Place nine drops of your first choice of a basic solution in well C2 and nine drops of your second choice of a base in C3. Rinse the pipette in distilled water after each addition.

3. Using the pipette, add 1 drop of the universal indicator to each of the wells C1–C3.

4. Observe the solution in each well. Record the solution and its color in **Table 2**.

5. Repeat steps 2–4 with your choices of acidic solution.

6. The color of the solutions in wells A1–A12 can be used to determine the pH of other solutions that are tested with the universal indicator. You can determine the pH of a solution by comparing its color with the color of the solution in wells A1–A12. Using **Table 1,** determine the pH values of the solutions that you tested in Part 1 of the procedure. Record the pH values in **Table 2**.

Part 2—Determining the pH of Solutions

Table 2

Solution	Color	pH

Going Further

Changes in the pH of blood and urine can be caused by illness. What are the normal pH values of human blood and urine? What illnesses can be detected by changes in these values? Investigate these questions, and write a report.

LAB 2 Inquiry Activity

Identifying Metals and Nonmetals

SCI 7.a. Students know how to identify regions corresponding to metals, nonmetals, and inert gases.

One property that distinguishes a metal from a nonmetal is electrical conductivity. Metals are good conductors of electricity because they have low resistance—electric current flows freely through them. Electrons carrying electric current are not blocked. Nonmetals generally are not good conductors, because they have high resistance. Resistance is caused when electrons strike atoms, making them vibrate. The flow of current is blocked causing the nonmetal to heat up.

Materials

- 1.5-V dry cell
- 3 insulated wires
- 1.5-V lamp
- electrical tape
- copper strip
- rubber sample
- wood sample
- unknown samples

What You'll Investigate

In this activity, you will construct a testing apparatus to determine whether various substances will conduct electricity. Identifying this property will help classify substances as metals or nonmetals.

Procedure

1. Use the Data and Observations Table to record your observations of the visual properties of each sample.

2. Use the wire, dry cell, lamp, and tape to construct a conductivity tester like the one in the drawing. Have your teacher check your set up.

3. Choose four unknown samples from the selection provided.

4. Predict if each sample is a metal or nonmetal. Write your prediction in the table.

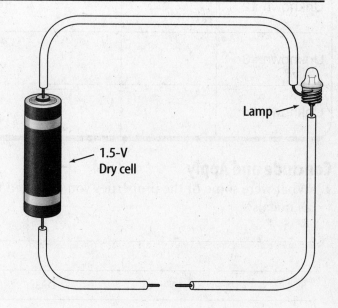

Lamp

1.5-V Dry cell

Data and Observations

Sample tested	Prediction	Visual observations	Metal	Nonmetal
Copper				
Wood				
Rubber				
Unknown #1				
Unknown #2				
Unknown #3				
Unknown #4				

Conclude and Apply

1. What were some of the properties you observed that were common to the samples you identified as metals?

_____

_____

_____

2. Was your unknown sample a metal or a nonmetal? What is your evidence?

_____

_____

_____

Going Further
List some of the ways the electrical conductivity of metals makes them useful. Then list some of the ways electrical conductivity can make it unsafe to use metals.

Inquiry Activity

Isotopes and Atomic Mass

SCI 3.a. Students know the structure of the atom and know it is composed of protons, neutrons, and electrons.

Atomic mass is the sum of the number of protons and the number of neutrons in the nucleus of an atom. All of the atoms of an element have the same number of protons in their nuclei, but the number of neutrons can be different. Atoms of the same element with different numbers of neutrons are called *isotopes.* Most elements have more than one isotope. Isotopes are identified by using the name of the element followed by the mass number of the isotope. For example, the three isotopes of hydrogen are hydrogen-1, or protium; hydrogen-2 , or deuterium; and hydrogen-3, or tritium. On a periodic table, the atomic mass given for each element is an average of the atomic mass of all the isotopes. This type of average is called a weighted average.

Materials

- 10 small plastic or paper cups
- black beans
- white beans
- calculator
- periodic table
- isotope table with color coding of stable isotopes

What You'll Investigate

In this activity, you will make models of the atomic nuclei of isotopes of the same element. You will use the atomic mass you determine from your models in approximately the same proportion as they occur in nature to find the weighted average atomic mass for the element.

Procedure

Part 1

1. Put 5 black beans in each of the cups. The black beans represent protons.
2. Put 5 white beans into two of the cups. Put 6 white beans in each of the remaining cups. The white beans represent neutrons.

3. Each cup represents an atom of this specific element. In **Table 1,** record the number of atoms represented and the mass number for each of the two isotopes.
4. Your teacher will help you calculate the average atomic mass for element A. Record this figure in **Table 1.**

Part 2

5. Empty the cups. Put 12 black beans in each.
6. Put 12 white beans in eight of the cups. Put 13 white beans in one of the remaining cups and 14 beans in the last cup.
7. Record in **Table 2** the number of atoms and mass number for each of the three isotopes.
8. Calculate the average atomic mass for element B. Record this figure in **Table 2.**

The Three Isotopes of Hydrogen

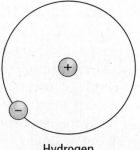

Hydrogen
atomic mass-1

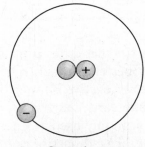

Deuterium
atomic mass-2

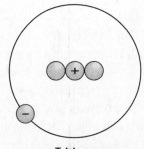

Tritium
atomic mass-3

Use what you learned in Parts 1 and 2 to complete Part 3.

Part 3

1. Model an element from the isotope table.
2. Follow the procedure for Parts 1 and 2 to set up a model for average atomic mass using the stable isotopes of your element.
3. Trade models with a different group.

4. Determine the number of stable isotopes involved and record the number of atoms and mass number for each.
5. Calculate the average atomic mass for the element, and identify it using the periodic table.
6. Meet with the other group and determine if you are correct. If not, work through their method with them to clarify and complete an error analysis.

Data and Observations

Table 1

Element A	Number of atoms	Mass number	Average atomic mass
Isotope 1			
Isotope 2			

Table 2

Element A	Number of atoms	Mass number	Average atomic mass
Isotope 1			
Isotope 2			
Isotope 3			

Conclude and Apply

1. Refer to your periodic table of the elements and identify the actual elements represented by A and B in this activity.

_____

_____

2. How do your calculations for the average atomic masses of these elements compare with those shown in the periodic table?

_____

_____

Going Further

Each isotope may have properties that differ from the properties of other isotopes. For example, some isotopes of normally nonradioactive elements are themselves radioactive. These radioactive isotopes are frequently used as *tracers* in animals and plants. Use research materials to find out what a tracer is and some isotopes that are commonly used as tracers. Explain why these isotopes are used as tracers and other radioactive isotopes may not be used.

Evaluating Solvents

SCI 3.d. Students know the states of matter (solid, liquid, gas) depend on molecular motion.

A solvent is a liquid in which a substance will dissolve and form a solution. Water is called a universal solvent because it is able to dissolve so many substances. The fact that water is a solvent for so many substances has advantages as well as disadvantages. Water in blood carries dissolved minerals and oxygen through the body—that's an advantage. However, water can also dissolve pollutants, such as fertilizer and pesticide run-off from farm fields, which can eventually make their way into our drinking water—that's a disadvantage.

Materials
- test-tube rack
- 8 test tubes and stoppers
- masking tape
- graduated cylinder
- 40 mL water
- 40 mL isopropyl alcohol
- 40 mL distilled water
- sugar, salt, citric acid, sand, powdered detergent, and styrofoam pellets

What You'll Investigate
In this activity, you will compare the ability of different liquids to dissolve certain solids.

Procedure

WARNING: *Isopropyl alcohol is flammable, an eye irritant, and has fumes. Citric acid is also an eye irritant.*

1. Brainstorm with your group about which solvent will be most effective at room temperature. List them in order of which can dissolve the most substances of those provided or which can dissolve the substances the fastest. Also, identify those solids that will be dissolved by one solvent but not by another.
2. Choose two solvents to compare. Label your first choice *A* and your second choice *B.*
3. Decide which four solids you will use to dissolve, or not, in the solvents. Label these as *a, b, c, d.*
4. Pour 10 mL of Solvent A into each of four test tubes marked *1–4.* Place the tubes in the test-tube rack.

5. Pour 10 mL of Solvent B into four test tubes marked *5–8.* Place the tubes in test-tube rack.
6. Place a pinch of Solid a in test tubes 1 and 5.
7. Place a pinch of Solid b in test tubes 2 and 6.
8. Place a pinch of Solid c in test tubes 3 and 7.
9. Place a pinch of Solid d in test tubes 4 and 8.
10. Cover each tube with a stopper, and shake.
11. Observe and record your results in the *Data and Observations* table.

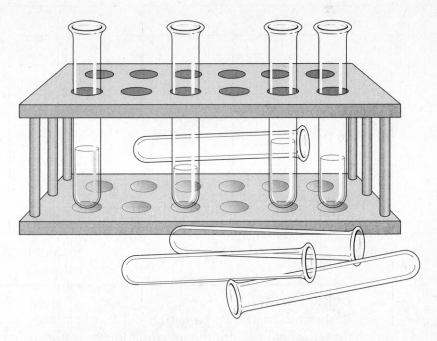

Data and Observations

Substance	Solvent A	Solvent B	Key
Solid a			
Solid b			++ dissolves entirely + partially dissolves 0 did not dissolve
Solid c			
Solid d			

Conclude and Apply

1. How did Solvent A compare to Solvent B in dissolving the four substances? In your explanation, include which dissolved the solid substances faster.

_____

_____

_____

_____

_____

Going Further
Research how acid precipitation illustrates the solvent abilities of water. How does the acid get into the precipitation?

LAB 5 Inquiry Activity

Chemical Reactions Based on pH Levels

SCI 5.a. Students know reactant atoms and molecules interact to form products with different chemical properties.

The pH of a solution can determine whether certain chemical reactions will take place. For example, the pH of milk affects the formation of curds in milk, as in the production of cottage cheese. The pH of a substance is measured by using indicators. Indicators change color to indicate whether a solution is acidic or basic. Acids have a pH of less than 7, and bases have a pH of more than 7. Pure water has a pH value of 7.0 and is considered neutral.

Materials

- pH paper
- vinegar
- lemon juice
- tea
- 50-mL graduated cylinder
- 40 mL milk
- 4 plastic cups
- stirring rod

What You'll Investigate

In this activity, you will observe the formation of curds in milk at different pH levels. You will determine what characteristic is common to the liquids that cause milk to curdle.

Procedure

WARNING: *Vinegar and the citric acid in lemon juice are eye irritants.*

1. Use pH paper to determine the pH of milk, and state if it is an acid, a base, or neutral.
2. Discuss how strong an acid would have to be to make the milk curdle. Decide how much of each acidic liquid would be needed to curdle the milk. Write this as a ratio.

3. Use the pH paper to determine the pH of the vinegar, lemon juice, and tea. Record these in the *Data and Observations* table.
4. Use the graduated cylinder to measure the predetermined amount of milk into each cup.
5. Thoroughly rinse the graduated cylinder and measure the vinegar as decided by group. Add it to the milk in one of the cups and stir. Observe carefully what happens to the milk. Record the results in the table.
6. Rinse the graduated cylinder and stirring rod. Repeat step 3 for each of the remaining solutions, using a separate cup of milk for each trial. Record your observations for each trial in the data table.

Copyright © Glencoe/McGraw-Hill, a division of The McGraw-Hill Companies, Inc.

Data and Observations

Solution	pH	Observations
Vinegar		
Lemon juice		
Tea		

Conclude and Apply

1. What did you observe happen to the milk with the addition of each solution?

_____

_____

2. What was the common factor for any of the solutions that caused the milk to curdle?

_____

_____

3. What do you think would happen if you changed the ratio of acid to milk?

_____

_____

Going Further

Why do you think certain solutions cause the milk to curdle? Name other reactions where the pH of a substance is important in determining whether a process or reaction will take place.

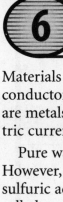

LAB 6 Inquiry Activity

Electrolytes and Conductivity

Materials that carry and electric current are called conductors. Generally, the best electric conductors are metals. That's because electrons that carry electric current can move freely through metals.

Pure water does not conduct an electric current. However, if a material such as sodium chloride or sulfuric acid is added to the water, the solution, called an *electrolyte,* will conduct electricity.

Materials
- metric ruler
- roll of household aluminum foil
- pencil
- 250-mL beaker
- 5 g table salt (sodium chloride)
- 100-mL beaker
- water
- stirring rod
- 2 flashlight batteries
- 4 wires
- bulb socket
- flashlight bulb
- masking tape
- 2 alligator clips

What You'll Investigate
In this activity, you will construct a simple conductivity tester and determine how electrodes affect the conductivity of an electrolyte.

Procedure

1. Make two electrodes by tearing two 15-cm lengths of aluminum foil from the roll. Carefully fold both lengthwise into 2-cm wide strips.
2. Use a pencil and metric ruler to mark 2-cm intervals along the length of one of the electrodes.
3. Securely fold the unmarked electrode over the side of the 250-mL beaker so that it touches the bottom of the beaker.
4. Place 5 g of sodium chloride into the 250-mL beaker. Add 200 mL of water to the beaker water and stir until the salt dissolves.
5. Set up the remaining materials as shown in **Figure 1.**
6. Momentarily touch the marked electrode to the top of the unmarked electrode and observe the flashlight bulb. Record your observations below.

_____

_____

_____

7. On the side of the beaker opposite the unmarked electrode, lower the marked electrode into the solution until 2 cm of it is submerged. Observe the flashlight bulb and record the observation in the *Data and Observations* table.
8. Repeat step 7 for submerged lengths of 4, 6, 8, and 10 cm.

Figure 1

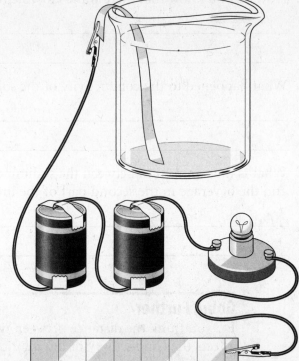

Data and Observations

Submerged length of electrode (cm)	Observations
2	
4	
6	
8	
10	

Part II

1. You have heard and read about athletes who drink certain beverages because of the electrolytes involved. Read the ingredients on the labels of two or three of these beverages.
2. Decide which beverage will give you the best use of your electrolytes. Explain.
3. Write a hypothesis related to the ingredients in one of the beverages and the probability that the beverage will conduct electricity.
4. Use the steps in the procedure in Part 1 to test your hypothesis.

Conclude and Apply

1. How do you know that there was a closed circuit in step 6?

_____

_____

2. What happened to the conductivity of the solution as the electrode was submerged? Explain.

_____

_____

3. What is the connection between the sodium chloride functioning as an electrolyte in the first part and the beverage in the second part of the investigation? Explain.

_____

_____

Going Further

Do you think the distance between two electrodes in a conducting solution affects the conductivity of the solution? Test your hypothesis.

Forensics Activities

Copyright © Glencoe/McGraw-Hill, a division of The McGraw-Hill Companies, Inc.

The Physics Final

The Problem

Luis is a senior in high school, and it is important that he score well on his physics final examination. A nearby college has accepted him for the next fall semester, as long as he earns a *B* or higher in all of his classes in the final marking period.

Luis is well prepared before the exam, knowing that he must earn at least an 80 percent in order to maintain a B average. Luis completes the exam in the time allowed and feels confident as he turns in his answer sheet. The exam is multiple choice, where the students fill in the circle next to each of their answer choices.

A problem develops when three of the answer sheets have no names on them. The scores on the answer sheets are 70 percent, 72 percent, and 87 percent. It is determined that Luis's answer sheet is one of them. Each of the answer sheets was completed in blue pen. The teacher quickly collects the pens in order to examine them and hopefully resolve the situation.

Your job is to make chromatograms from the three pens and compare them to the chromatograms made from the three answer sheets.

Pen A belongs to Student 1.

Pen B belongs to Student 2.

Pen C belongs to Luis.

Background

Compounds Compounds form when two or more elements combine chemically. Each different compound has a different combination of elements and atoms in its particles. Each compound also has a different set of properties, such as color and solubility. Compounds have different properties because of the different kinds of elements and different ratios of their atoms in a compound.

Inks and Pigments Inks contain pigments. A pigment is a compound that absorbs some colors of light and reflects others. The color you see is the color of light reflected by the pigment. Different brands of an ink color such as black contain different mixtures of pigments.

Solubility The ability of a substance to dissolve is solubility. Different compounds have different

degrees of solubility in a solvent. This means that solubility can be used to separate a mixture of compounds. Have you noticed how ink often runs when the paper it is on gets wet? This is because the ink is soluble in water. As water moves through the paper, some of the ink dissolves and is carried with the water. Different dissolved pigments move at different rates, depending on the solvent and the kind of paper used.

Chromatography The solubility of different compounds can be used to separate a mixture of compounds. This process is called *chromatography*. Filter paper is one material that is used for chromatography. After chromatography, spots of different colors can be found at different places along the paper. Each strip is called a chromatogram.

SCI 3.b. Students know that compounds are formed by combining two or more different elements and that compounds have properties that are different from their constituent elements. Also covers **SCI 7.c.**

Everyday Materials

❑ pens labeled *A*, *B*, and *C*

Lab Materials

❑ three strips of chromatography paper
❑ scissors
❑ metric ruler
❑ pencil

❑ 150 mL beaker
❑ three chromatograms labeled 70%, 72%, and 87%
❑ solvent
❑ paper towels

Safety

- Do not inhale vapors or taste, touch, or smell any chemical or substance.
- Always wear safety goggles and a lab apron.
- Wash your hands thoroughly after each lab activity.

Procedure

1. Put on your lab apron and safety goggles, and wear them for the entire experiment.

2. Using Pen A, make a circular mark about 3 cm from the end of one of the strips. Your circle should be filled in, and its diameter (distance across) should be about 0.5 cm. Write *Pen A* across the top of your strip; this label should be on the end opposite your circular mark.

3. Repeat step 2 with Pen B and Pen C, using a different strip for each pen.

4. Take the strip for Pen A. Make a fold in the strip 5 cm from the end of the strip (on the end where the label is located).

5. Repeat step 4 for the Pen B and Pen C strips.

6. Place the strip from Pen A on the edge of the beaker. The fold should prevent the strip from falling inside. Slowly pour the solvent in the beaker until it reaches a point on the strip just *below* the ink dot. It is important that the solvent reaches the bottom of the paper but does not touch the ink dot. Refer to the illustration of the setup for help.

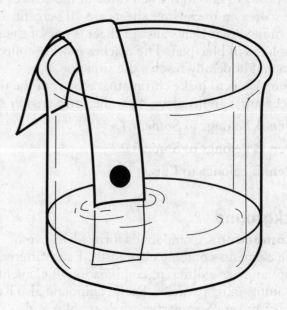

Leave the paper in the solvent for about 5 minutes, or until the paper is no longer absorbing the solvent. Observe what happens to the ink spot as the paper absorbs the solvent.

7. Remove the strip from the beaker, and place the strip in a safe place to dry.

8. Repeat step 6 and step 7 for the strip from Pen B and the strip from Pen C.

9. When all three strips are dry, neatly tape them to a sheet of paper.

10. Clean up as directed by your teacher, and answer the questions that follow.

Forensics Activity 1 (continued)

Conclude and Apply

1. Explain why different chemical compounds behave differently during chromatography.

   _____

   _____

   _____

2. How do you think covering the spots of ink with solvent might affect your results?

   _____

   _____

   _____

3. You were instructed to leave the paper in the solution until the paper no longer absorbs the solution. Why is this important?

   _____

   _____

   _____

4. What information about the pens and ink are you assuming?

   _____

   _____

   _____

Analyze and Conclude

5. Compare your chromatograms to the chromatograms from the three answer sheets. Did Luis maintain his B average after the final exam? Explain.

   _____

   _____

   _____

   _____

   _____

Forensics Activity 1 (continued)

6. Could you have matched each student with the correct answer sheet if all three students had used the same kind of pen? Explain.

_____

_____

_____

_____

_____

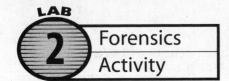

The Case of the Sabotaged Boat Race

The Problem

There is controversy surrounding the annual eighth grade "Design the Fastest Boat" contest. Each of the five participants was given the supplies listed below to build their boats.

- 0.6 L plastic drink bottles (green or clear) with caps (2)
- small wooden dowels
- instant glue
- tape
- square of fabric (10 cm by 10 cm)

- cardboard
- small weights
- safety pin
- paper clip
- plastic propeller
- rubber band

Boats 3, 4, and 5 get off to a quick start, but Boats 1 and 2 are noticeably slower than the rest. Early on in the race, Boat 2 actually sinks. Boat 1 does make it to the finish line, although it is far behind Boats 3, 4, and 5. No one is sure what happened to Boat 2; it cannot be retrieved from the bottom of the river.

The designers of Boat 1 and Boat 2 want to find out what happened to them. The two students have filed a complaint with the organizer of the race.

Boat Owner 1: "I left my boat alone for a few minutes before the race. Then I returned and put my boat in the water. My boat felt heavier than it had before I left, but the race was starting and I had to get my boat in the water. After the race started, I found an empty bottle of corn oil nearby. While I was gone, I think someone uncapped the bottles in my boat, filled each one with corn oil, and then recapped them. I think the corn oil was the reason my boat came in fourth place."

Boat Owner 2: "Before the race started, someone I didn't recognize came up to me. She handed me a bottle that said "corn syrup" and told me that if I poured it into my bottles, it would make my boat faster. I know that we weren't supposed to use any additional materials, but this mystery girl was so convincing that I went ahead and did it. She probably was helping out one of the three boats that quickly finished the race. I think the corn syrup made my boat sink."

Your job is to decide what happened to the boats. In addition to examining the statements, you will also build your own boat to simulate what took place during the race.

Background

Buoyancy Have you ever been underwater and picked up a heavy rock? Did it seem lighter in the water than in the air? Water exerts a *buoyant force* on objects. A buoyant force acts in an upward direction against gravity, making an object feel lighter in water.

Sink or float? There always is a downward force on a submerged object. This is the object's weight. If the weight of the object is greater than the buoyant force, then the object will sink. If the weight of the object is less than the buoyant force, the object will float.

 SCI 8.d. Students know how to predict whether an object will float or sink.

Forensics Activity 2 (continued)

Density If you examine a bottle of oil and vinegar salad dressing that has not been shaken, you will notice that the oil floats on top of the vinegar. This is because the liquids have different densities. Water has a density of 1 g/cm^3. Liquids with densities greater than water sink, while liquids with densities less than water float.

Everyday Materials

❏ corn syrup
❏ corn oil

Lab Materials

❏ 0.6 L plastic drink bottles with caps (2)
❏ small wooden dowels
❏ instant glue
❏ tape
❏ square of fabric (10 cm × 10 cm)

❏ cardboard
❏ small weights
❏ safety pin
❏ paper clip
❏ plastic propeller
❏ rubber band
❏ large tub of water

Safety

- Do not inhale vapors or taste, touch, or smell any chemical or substance unless told to do so by your teacher.
- Always wear safety goggles and a lab apron.
- Wash your hands thoroughly after each lab activity.

Procedure

1. Put on your lab apron and safety goggles, and wear them for the entire experiment.

2. Before starting to build your boat, discuss design plans with the members of your group. Examine the boat your teacher has made.

When everyone agrees on the plan, start to build your boat. You do not have to use all the materials on the list. Boat designs among different groups can vary.

3. Test your boat in the tub of water to make sure it floats. If so, move on to the next step. If your boat does not float, repeat the previous step until it does.

4. Use your boat to test each of the two conditions described in the boat owners' statements. Be sure to completely clean the bottles before adding a new liquid to them. Record your observations in the data table on the next page.

5. Clean up your workspace as directed by your teacher, then complete the following questions.

Forensics Activity 2 (continued)

Data and Observations

	Boat 1	Boat 2
Describe the student's claim.		
Would this cause the boat to slow or sink?		
Explain. Be sure to include *buoyancy*, *weight*, and *density* in your response.		

Conclude and Apply

1. Explain why some objects float while others sink.

_____

_____

_____

2. Why were you instructed to leave the caps on the bottles?

_____

_____

_____

3. What do you think would have happened if you had not left on the caps?

_____

_____

_____

4. Besides their density properties, why do you think corn oil and corn syrup were used to sabotage the boats?

_____

_____

Forensics Activity 2 (continued)

Analyze and Conclude

5. After examining the statements and simulating the race conditions, describe what happened to Boat 1 and Boat 2 in the race.

_____

_____

_____

_____

_____

6. Could the boats have sunk if someone had not tampered with them? Explain.

_____

_____

_____

Who released Jumbo?

SCI 1.a. Students know position is defined in relation to some choice of a standard reference point and a set of reference directions. Also covers **SCI 1.c.**

The Problem

Fridays are pep rally days at Central Middle School. This Friday is a special day for the Bulldogs. The school mascot, a bulldog named Jumbo, is on campus for the noon pep rally. Ms. B, the mascot's owner, has dropped Jumbo at the school on her way to work. After his morning walk through the hallways, the principal, Mr. S, returns to the main office. He notices that Jumbo's crate is empty. Mr. S knows the crate was securely shut beforehand, so he suspects that a student might have taken the dog as a prank.

To his relief, Mr. S quickly finds the dog in the hallway leading to the gym. Mr. S calls Ms. B to let her know what happened, even though Jumbo has been secured. He is surprised by Ms. B's reaction; she is upset and wants to know how Jumbo was released from his crate. If this turns out to be a prank, Ms. B wants the culprit identified and disciplined by the school.

Mr. S wants to resolve the issue as soon as possible, so he begins the investigation, collecting statements from a computer teacher, an attendance person, and a librarian. He discovers that three students were not accounted for at the time of the disappearance.

Mr. S: "I left the main office at 9:00 A.M. to make my usual rounds. Jumbo was in his crate when I left, but she was gone when I returned at 9:05 A.M. I found Jumbo in the hallway leading to the gym. I saw no students running in the hallways."

Ms. B: "I left Jumbo in her crate in the main office at 8:55 A.M., just as the bell was ringing for the second period class."

Computer teacher: "One of my students (**Suspect A**) left my room at 9:02 A.M. to go to the bathroom. He returned to the computer room at 9:05 A.M."

Attendance person: "One student (**Suspect B**) arrived late to school. She checked in at the attendance office at 9:00 A.M. Her math teacher told me she arrived at her classroom at 9:05 A.M."

Librarian: "One student (**Suspect C**) came to the library with a pass. I signed her pass at 9:04 A.M., but I noticed her science teacher wrote the pass at 9:00 A.M."

Your job is to determine if any of the students had time to release Jumbo from his crate.

Background

Constant Speed and Instantaneous

Speed Constant speed involves moving exactly the same distance in each unit of time measured. The speed of a moving object at any given point in time is its instantaneous speed.

Average Speed Most objects do not move at a constant speed for a long period of time. Along a moving object's path, its instantaneous speed will probably change many times, so average speed is used to describe an object's overall speed. To find average speed, divide the total distance between two points by the total time it took to travel that distance.

$$\text{average speed} = \frac{\text{total distance}}{\text{total time}}$$

Using Formulas You can solve for average speed if you know the total distance and total time. You can also solve for either total distance or time if you know the other two measurements. For example:

$$\text{total time} = \frac{\text{total distance}}{\text{average speed}}$$

$$\text{total distance} = \frac{\text{average speed}}{\text{total time}}$$

Forensics Activity 3 (continued)

Before you decide which formula to use, determine which measurements you have. Then choose the formula that solves for the unknown information you need.

Everyday Materials

❏ pencil
❏ paper

Lab Materials

❏ stopwatch, or clock
❏ calculator
❏ meter stick

Safety

- Use caution when handling the compass.
- Always wear safety goggles and a lab apron.
- Wash your hands thoroughly after each lab activity.

Procedure

1. Put on your lab apron and safety goggles, and wear them for the entire experiment.

2. The organization chart below shows the layout of the rooms and the distance between them in meters. Use the table on the next page to identify two routes for each suspect. For the first route, assume the suspect did not commit the prank. For the second route, assume the suspect did commit the prank. The routes for Suspect A have been done for you.

3. Determine the total distance each suspect would have to walk to finish each possible route. Use the measurements in the chart to find each distance. Record the total distances in the table.

4. Use the members of your group to estimate the average walking speed of an eighth-grader. To do this, take turns timing how long it takes each member to briskly walk 10 meters. Calculate the average walking speed of each member of your group. Then find the average of the average speeds. Record your results below.

Average walking speed: _____

5. Find the total amount of time each suspect had to commit the prank. Be sure to find the total amount of time in seconds, not minutes. The time for Suspect A has been done for you. Record this information in the table.

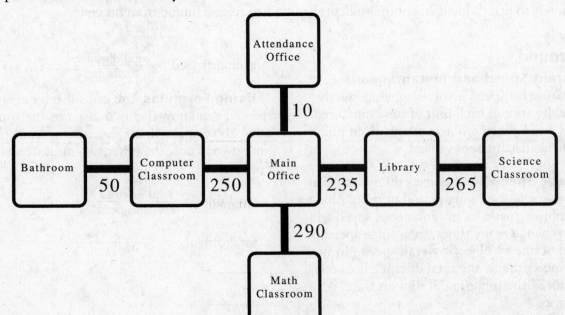

Forensics Activity 3 (continued)

6. Find the total distance covered in each route. Record this information in the table.

7. Calculate the average speed for each suspect on each possible route. Record this information in the table.

8. Compare the average speed on each possible route for each suspect with the average walking speed of an eighth-grader. Record *yes* or *no* in the table to show if each suspect could be the culprit.

Data and Observations

Suspect	Possible Routes	Total Time Available (s)	Total Distance (m)	Average Speed (m/s)	Culprit?
A	computer room to bathroom and back	180			
	computer room to main office and back				
B					
C					

Conclude and Apply

1. Why did you work with average speed instead of instantaneous speed?

_____

_____

_____

Forensics Activity 3 (continued)

2. You found the average walking speed of your group and used this to estimate the average walking speed of the suspect. Is it safe to assume that your group's average walking speed is close to that of the suspect? Explain.

_____

_____

_____

Analyze and Conclude

3. Based on your observations and calculations, which student could have been responsible for releasing Jumbo? Continue to assume the student walked briskly. Explain your reasoning.

_____

_____

_____

_____

4. If you had to defend the suspect you named in question 3, what other factors would you consider that might be helpful to your case? Explain.

_____

_____

_____

_____

5. The velocity of an object is the speed of the object and direction of its motion. Think of a real-life situation where velocity might be important in a court case. Describe your scenario.

_____

_____

_____

_____

49er Fever

The Problem

A man takes a two-week trip sponsored by 49er Fever, LLC, which runs prospecting adventures. Before signing up for the trip, 49er Fever guarantees he will discover gold and/or diamonds on his adventure. The man is skeptical about the company's claim but decides to give it a try.

The man returns home with an impressive amount of what appear to be gold and diamonds. He is still skeptical of the company's claim, so he wants to have the minerals tested. The man will consider suing the company for false advertisement if the minerals do not turn out to be genuine gold and diamonds.

You have been hired by the man to examine and identify his collected samples.

Background

Minerals are inorganic solids found naturally in Earth's crust. They have a regular crystalline pattern. Scientists have identified over 3,000 different minerals. Identifying these minerals can be a challenging process. Scientists and students use several properties to help them identify minerals. Two of the most useful properties are hardness and density. The table on the next page describes three properties of some common minerals.

Hardness The hardness of a mineral is a measure of its resistance to scratching. The hardness of an unknown mineral can be determined by scratching it against minerals on the Mohs Hardness Scale. The scale lists ten minerals in order of increasing hardness. Talc is the softest mineral, with a hardness of 1; diamond is the hardest mineral, with a hardness of 10. It is not always possible to have a complete set of minerals for comparison. The following common objects can be used for this purpose:

- fingernail: hardness of 2.5
- copper penny: hardness of 3.0
- steel nail: hardness of 5.5
- glass: hardness of 6.5

You can use a scratch test to estimate the hardness of an object. For example, an object that can be scratched by a steel nail but not by a penny has a hardness between 3.0 and 5.5.

Density The density of a mineral is a useful property. Density is the ratio of the mass of a substance to its volume. If you want to know the density of an unknown mineral, weigh it first, then add a known volume of water to a graduated cylinder. Add the mineral to the water in the graduated cylinder, and note the new volume. Subtract the original volume from this number to determine the volume of water displaced by the mineral, which is also the volume of the mineral itself.

The density of a mineral can be found using the following formula:

$$\text{density} = \frac{\text{mass of mineral}}{\text{volume of water displaced by mineral}}$$

SCI 7.c. Students know substances can be classified by their properties, including their melting temperature, density, hardness, and thermal and electrical conductivity.

Forensics Activity 4 (continued)

Mineral	Hardness	Density (g/cm³)	Colors
Gold	3.5	19.3	pale yellow, brown, gray, white, blue, black, reddish, greenish, colorless
Orthoclase	6.0	2.53 to 2.56	off-white, yellow, shades of red, orange to brown
Topaz	8.0	2.6	colorless, white, colored
Diamond	10.0	3.5	pale yellow, brown, gray, white, blue, black, reddish, greenish, colorless

Everyday Materials

❏ water
❏ copper penny
❏ steel nail
❏ small piece of glass

Lab Materials

❏ four unknown minerals (samples 1 through 4) from the 49er trip

❏ 100 mL graduated cylinder
❏ balance
❏ samples of gold, orthoclase, topaz, and diamond

Safety

- Always wear safety goggles and a lab apron.
- Wash your hands thoroughly after each lab activity.
- Be careful when handling glass.

Procedure

1. Put on your lab apron and safety goggles, and wear them for the entire experiment.

2. Use your fingernail, copper penny, steel nail, glass, and your samples of gold, orthoclase, topaz, and diamond to approximate the hardness of unknown samples 1 through 4. Record your results in the table.

3. Working with one sample at a time, place each of the unknown samples on the scale and record its mass in the table.

4. Fill the graduated cylinder to 30 mL. Working with one unknown sample at a time, add the sample to the graduated cylinder. Measure the volume of water that the sample displaces. Record your results in the table.

5. Calculate the density of each unknown sample. Record your results in the table.

6. Clean up your workstation as directed by your teacher, then answer the questions that follow.

Forensics Activity 4 (continued)

Data and Observations

Sample	Hardness	Mass	Volume of Water Displaced	Density (g/cm³)
1				
2				
3				
4				

Conclude and Apply

1. List the hardness of unknown samples 1 through 4. Briefly describe how you approximated them.

_____

_____

_____

_____

2. Suppose you have a mineral sample and your partner has a smaller sample of the same mineral. Would the density calculations for the samples be different? Explain.

_____

_____

_____

_____

3. Suppose you have two different mineral samples. The volumes of the two samples are similar, but the densities of the samples are not. Describe how you could compare the densities of the two samples if you had no access to lab equipment.

_____

_____

_____

Forensics Activity 4 (continued)

4. Describe the colors of the unknown samples 1 through 4.

_____

_____

Analyze and Conclude

5. Based on your investigations and calculations, did the man find any gold or diamonds? Explain your reasoning.

_____

_____

_____

_____

_____

6. Do you think the man has a legitimate claim against 49er Fever? Explain.

_____

_____

_____

_____

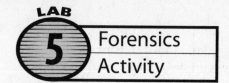

LAB 5 — Forensics Activity

Who served the botulism?

The Problem

The town of Franklin held its annual Town Dinner as usual this year. Unfortunately, this one will long be remembered as the "botulism dinner." At least 20 people became sick with botulism. The organizers wish they had paid closer attention to food preparation, and the people who donated to the dinner felt awful because they did not know if they were the culprits.

As usual, the dinner was held in February when people could use a break from the winter. Much of the food served was canned by the local citizens in the late summer and early fall as the last of the gardens were harvested. Some people used pressure cookers to can their foods, while others did not.

The local board of health interviewed all the people who had become ill. It has been determined that they each ate at least some of the following foods:

- Mr. B's canned corn
- Mrs. C's canned corn
- Mr. D's canned tomatoes
- Ms. E's canned tomatoes

The board then interviewed each of the four people named above. These were their responses when asked about their canning preparations.

Mr. B: "I canned the corn from my garden. I used a hot-water bath during the canning this year. Last year, my pressure cooker almost exploded on me, and I wasn't going to risk that again."

Mrs. C: "We had a great crop of corn this year, so I was glad to donate some of it to the Town Dinner. I always use a pressure cooker when I can my corn. That is the way my grandmother taught me."

Mr. D: "I had prepared tomatoes for the dinner. I used a hot-water bath. I think I read somewhere that tomatoes don't need a pressure cooker. I hope that was right, because I would feel awful if I poisoned all those people!"

Ms. E: "I just bought one of those new pressure cookers—the kind that doesn't explode. I canned all my tomatoes with it this year. It was very quick and easy."

Your job is to determine which of these foods caused the botulism outbreak at the Town Dinner.

Background

Botulism The symptons of botulism usually develop within 6 hours to 2 weeks (most commonly from 12 to 36 hours) after eating toxin-containing food. Symptoms of botulism include double vision, blurred vision, drooping eyelids, slurred speech, difficulty swallowing, dry mouth, and muscle weakness. Botulism is a serious illness caused by a nerve toxin that is produced by the bacterium *Clostridium botulinum*.

Many cases of botulism have come from home-canned foods with low acid content, such as asparagus, green beans, and beets. Pressure cookers should be used to can foods with low acid content; this prevents the growth of bacteria that can lead to botulism.

SCI 5.e. Students know how to determine whether a solution is acidic, basic, or neutral.

Forensics Activity 5 (continued)

Acidic Foods An acid is a substance that tastes sour, reacts with metals and carbonates, and turns blue litmus paper red. Foods that taste sour or tart are usually high in acid content. Lemons, grapefruits, oranges, and limes all contain citric acid. Other foods such as apples, vinegar, tea, and sour milk are acidic as well. High-temperature baths can be used to can foods with high acid content.

Everyday Materials

- ❏ ear of corn
- ❏ tomato
- ❏ water
- ❏ plastic knife
- ❏ paper towels

Lab Materials

- ❏ mortar and pestle
- ❏ pH test strips
- ❏ two small 50-mL beakers
- ❏ stirring rod

Safety

- Handle the plastic knife carefully.
- Always wear safety goggles and a lab apron.
- Wash your hands thoroughly after each lab activity.
- Never eat or drink anything in the lab.

Procedure

1. Put on your lab apron and safety goggles, and wear them for the entire experiment.

2. Cut off a small piece of corn from the corncob.

3. Grind the corn in the mortar and pestle, and transfer the crushed corn to the beaker. Add a small amount of water to make a slurry of corn.

4. Use a pH test strip to determine the pH of the corn. Place the value in the table below.

5. Clean the mortar and pestle with a paper towel.

6. Repeat steps 2–4 for the tomato.

7. Read the instructions to the pressure cooker, then review the interviews from the cooks. Complete the data table.

8. Clean up as directed by your teacher and answer the questions that follow.

Data and Observations

Cook	Food	pH of Food	How was it canned?	Cause of botulism?
Mr. B	corn			
Mrs. C	corn			
Mr. D	tomatoes			
Ms. E	tomatoes			

Forensics Activity 5 (continued)

Conclude and Apply

1. What is the benefit of using a pressure cooker? What are the potential drawbacks?

_____

_____

_____

_____

_____

2. What is the pH of tomatoes? What is the pH of corn? Which is more acidic, tomatoes or corn?

_____

_____

_____

_____

_____

3. Which foods should be cooked in a pressure cooker? Which foods are safe to can in a hot-water bath? Explain.

_____

_____

_____

_____

_____

_____

Analyze and Conclude

4. Based on the interviews and your data collection, which food caused the outbreak of botulism? Explain how you know.

_____

_____

_____

_____

_____

Forensics Activity 5 (continued)

5. Describe at least one step the town could take to avoid a similar outbreak in the future.

_____

_____

_____

_____

_____

6. This lab involves food-borne botulism caused by improperly preserving or storing food. There are two other ways that botulism can be transmitted. Research the two ways, then write a brief description of each one.

_____

_____

_____

_____

_____

Probeware Activities

Getting Started with Probeware

The following instructions will guide you through the setup process for the data collection unit and the graphing calculator. The activities are compatible with either the CBL 2 or the LabPro unit. Each activity was written for use with TI-73 or TI-83 Plus graphing calculators. These activities can be adapted for use with other graphing calculators or other data collection units, if desired.

Connecting a Graphing Calculator to the CBL 2 or LabPro Unit

1. Insert batteries into the CBL 2 or LabPro unit and graphing calculator.

2. The cradle is an optional accessory that conveniently connects the two units. Slide the back of the cradle onto the front of the CBL 2 or LabPro unit until it clicks into place.

3. Insert the upper end of the calculator into the cradle and press down on the lower end until it locks into place.

4. Connect the CBL 2 or LabPro unit to the graphing calculator using the unit-to-unit link cable. Plug the cable into the I/O port at the end of the CBL 2 or LabPro unit and the other end into the I/O port at the end of the calculator. Make sure that the unit-to-unit link cable is securely in place.

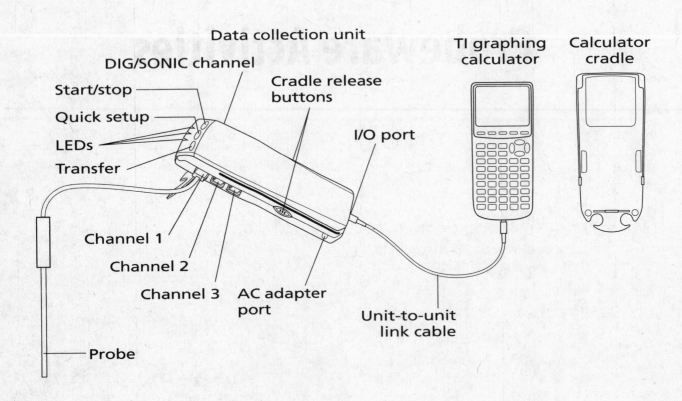

Resetting the Calculator Memory

It is recommended that the memory of the calculator be cleared before the DataMate data collection program is transferred.

1. Press ⌐2nd⌐ [**MEM**].

2. Select **Reset.**

3. Select **ALL RAM…**

4. Select **Reset.** The calculator screen
   will display **RAM cleared.**

Transferring DataMate to the Calculator

The DataMate program is stored on the CBL 2 or LabPro unit and is transferred to the graphing calculator for use. Once DataMate is transferred to the graphing calculator, it will remain there until the calculator memory is reset using the instructions above.

1. For the TI-73, press ⌐APPS⌐. Select **Link…**

   For the TI-83 Plus, press ⌐2nd⌐ [**LINK**].

2. Use the right arrow to highlight **RECEIVE.** Press ⌐ENTER⌐.

3. The screen will display **Waiting…** Press the large **TRANSFER** key found on the upper left-hand side of the CBL 2 or LabPro unit. When the transfer is complete, the screen will display the transferred programs followed by the word **Done.**

4. Press ⌐2nd⌐ [**QUIT**].

Starting DataMate

When you are ready to collect data, use the following instructions to start DataMate.

For the TI-73:

1. Press ⌐PRGM⌐.

2. Select **DataMate.**

3. Press ⌐ENTER⌐.

For the TI-83 Plus:

1. Press ⌐APPS⌐.

2. Select **DataMate.**

Setting up Probes Manually

The CBL 2 and LabPro unit should recognize the probe attached automatically. If this does not happen, follow these instructions.

1. Select **SETUP** from the DataMate main screen.

2. Press ⌐ENTER⌐ to select channel 1, or select the channel where the probe is inserted.

3. Select the correct sensor number from the SELECT SENSOR menu.

4. If requested, select the type of probe used.

5. Select **OK** to return to the DataMate main screen.

Using the TI-73 Graphing Calculator to Create a Histogram

A histogram is a graph that shows data divided into equal ranges and the number of data points that fall into each range. The following instructions explain how to make a histogram for the heart rate data in *Exercise and Heart Rate*.

1. **Resetting Calculator Memory** Turn on your graphing calculator and press [2nd] [**MEM**]. Select **Clr All Lists**. Press [ENTER].

2. **Creating and Entering Data Into Lists** Press [LIST] to access an empty data table. Name your lists before entering data. Scroll up to the title bar (the "top shelf") and over to the first empty list beyond L6 (lists L1–L6 cannot be renamed). Press [2nd] [**TEXT**]. Scroll to the desired letters, pressing [ENTER] after each. Choose a title of 5 or fewer letters. Then scroll down to **DONE**. Press [ENTER] twice to title your new list. Repeat for the other two variables. Enter your class data in all three lists.

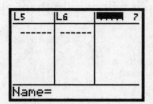 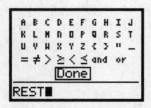 

3. **Setting up Graphs** Press [2nd] [**PLOT**]. Select **Plot 1** by pressing [ENTER]. Use the arrow keys and [ENTER] to turn the plot on and to select the sixth graph icon, a histogram. For the Xlist, press [2nd] [LIST] and scroll down to find the resting heart rate list. Press [ENTER] twice. Ignore Freq.

 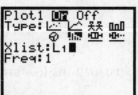 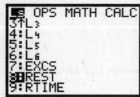 

4. Repeat **Step 3** to set up Plot 2 and Plot 3, but do not turn them ON yet. The Xlists will be your exercise heart rate and recovery time lists.

5. **Plotting Data** Press [ZOOM]. Then select **ZoomStat** to see your first histogram for resting heart rate. Use the [TRACE] and arrow keys to find the heart rate range that occurred in the class most often and the number of students that were in this range.

6. Press [2nd] [**PLOT**] to turn off Plot 1, and turn on Plot 2. Repeat step 5 for Plot 3 to see the class histogram for exercise heart rate and recovery time.

 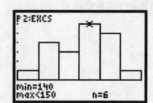 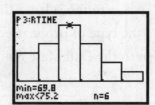

Using the TI-83 Plus Graphing Calculator to Create a Histogram

1. **Resetting Calculator Memory** Turn on your graphing calculator and press [2nd] **[MEM].** Select **Clr All Lists.** Press [ENTER].

2. **Creating and Entering Data into Lists** Name your lists before entering data. Press [STAT] and select **Edit.** Scroll up to the title bar (the "top shelf") and over to the first empty list beyond L6 (lists L1–L6 cannot be renamed). The highlighted "A" in the upper corner indicates that you are already in locked-alpha mode. Find and press the desired letters on the keypad. Press [ENTER] to title your new list for the resting heart rate data. Repeat for exercise heart rate and recovery time. Choose abbreviations that make sense to you—the names are limited to five letters. Enter all data.

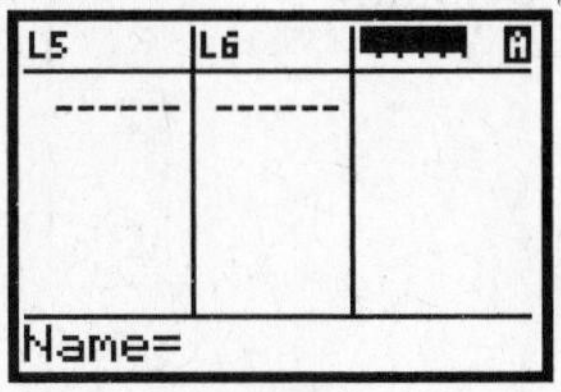

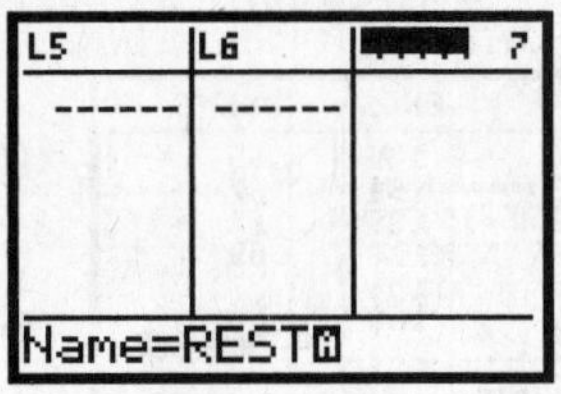

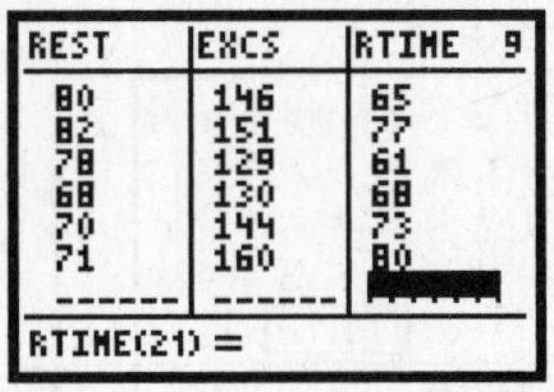

3. **Setting up Graphs** Set up your calculator for graphing your data. Press [2nd] **[STAT PLOT].** Select **Plot 1** by pressing [ENTER]. Use the arrow keys and [ENTER] to turn the plot on and select the third graph icon, a histogram. For the Xlist, press [2nd] [LIST] and scroll down to find your resting heart rate list. Press [ENTER] twice. Leave Freq. at 1.

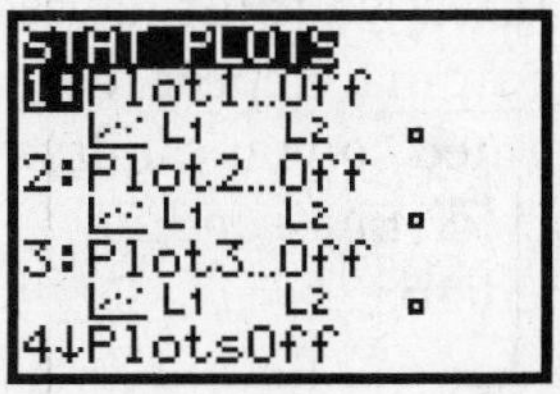

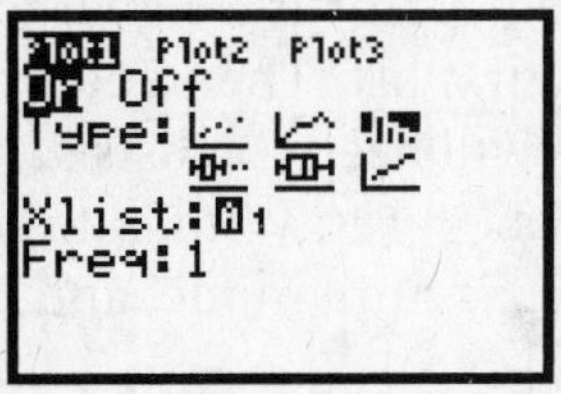

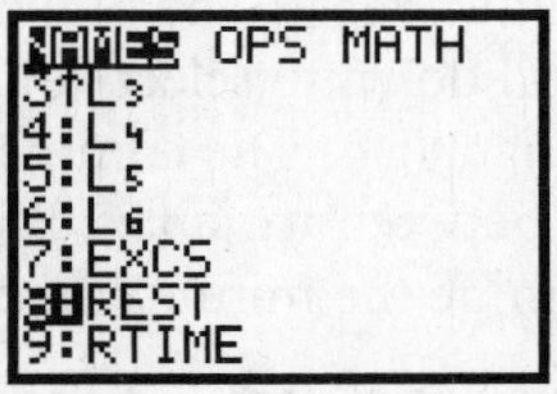

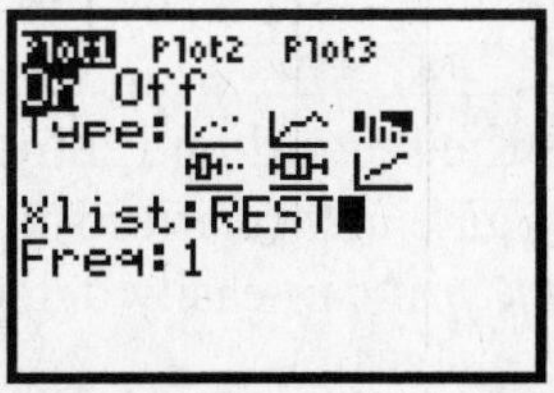

4. Repeat **Step 3** to set up Plot 2 and then Plot 3, but do not turn Plot 2 and Plot 3 ON yet. The Xlists will be your exercise heart rate and recovery time lists.

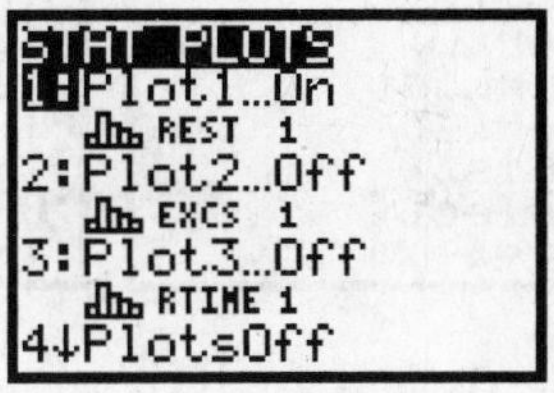

5. **Plotting Data** Press [ZOOM]. Then select **ZoomStat** to see the first histogram, for resting heart rate. Use the [TRACE] and arrow keys to find the heart rate range that occurred in the class most often and the number of students that were in this range.

6. Press [2nd] [STAT] **[PLOT]** to turn off Plot 1, and turn on Plot 2. Press [ZOOM]. Then select **ZoomStat** again to see the class histogram for exercise heart rate. Then turn off Plot 2 and turn on Plot 3 to see the class histogram for recovery time.

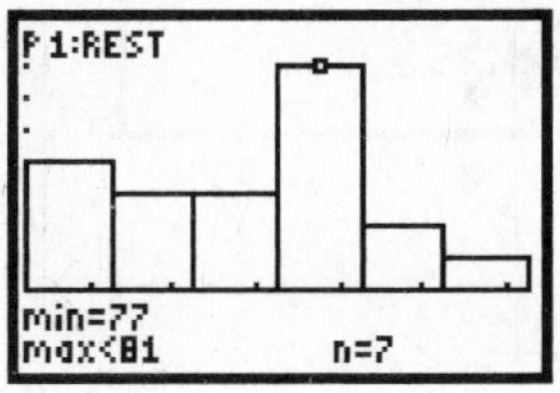

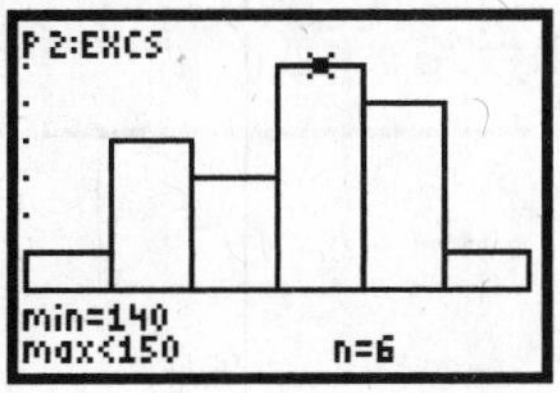

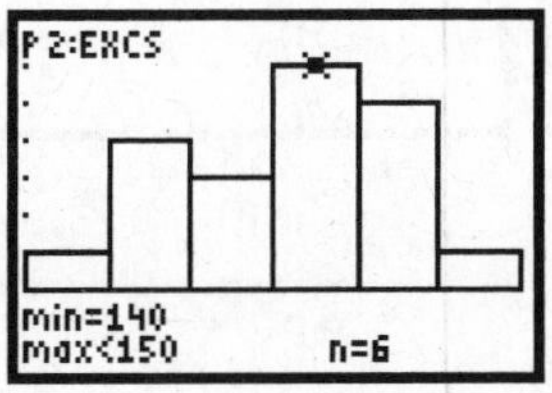

Using the TI-73 Graphing Calculator to Create a Box Plot and Display Statistics

Note: If you have already used the calculator to make histograms, skip to step #4.

1. **Resetting Calculator Memory** Turn on your graphing calculator and press ⟨2nd⟩ [**MEM**]. Select **Clr All Lists.** Press ⟨ENTER⟩.

2. Press ⟨LIST⟩ to access an empty data table. Name your lists before entering data. Scroll up to the title bar (the "top shelf") and over to the first empty list beyond L6 (lists L1–L6 cannot be renamed). Press ⟨2nd⟩ [**TEXT**]. Use the arrow keys to select the desired letters, pressing ⟨ENTER⟩ after each. List names are limited to five letters. Go to **DONE** when you are finished entering the name. Press ⟨ENTER⟩ twice to title your new list for the resting heart rate data.

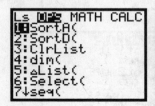 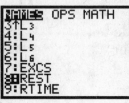 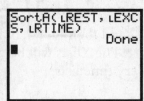

3. Repeat for the other two variables, choosing abbreviations for exercise heart rate and recovery time with 5 or fewer letters. Enter your class data in all three lists.

4. Order the data in your lists. Press ⟨2nd⟩ [**STAT**]. Use the right arrow key to select **OPS.** Select the default, **Sort A,** by pressing ⟨ENTER⟩. The blinking cursor is a signal to insert your list names. Press ⟨2nd⟩ ⟨LIST⟩ and scroll down to select your first list. Then enter a comma. Repeat to select the second and third data lists. The commas will keep the lists separated so you can later investigate any relationship between variables. Press ⟨ENTER⟩. With data sorted (in ascending order), you can easily determine the minimum, maximum, mode, and median.

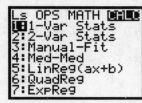 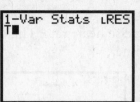 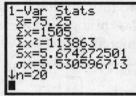 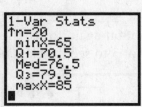

5. For statistical analysis, access the one-variable statistics for each list. Press ⟨2nd⟩ [**STAT**]. Use the right arrow key to select **CALC.** Select the default, **1–Var Stats.** Press ⟨ENTER⟩. Press ⟨2nd⟩ ⟨LIST⟩ to retrieve one of your lists. Press ⟨ENTER⟩. The mean (x̄) is the first entry. Scroll down to find the minimum (minX), median (Med), and maximum (maxX).

6. Set up your calculator for graphing your data. Press [2nd] [**PLOT**]. Select the default, **Plot 1,** by pressing [ENTER]. Use the arrow keys and [ENTER] to turn the plot on and select the seventh graph icon, a standard box plot. For the Xlist, press [2nd] [LIST] and scroll down to find your resting heart rate list. Press [ENTER] twice. Leave Freq. at 1.

 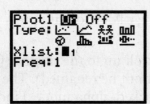 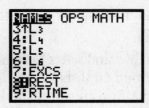 

7. Repeat **Step 5** to set up and turn on Plot 2 and then Plot 3. The Xlists will be your exercise heart rate and recovery time lists. Because the data for all three lists is in the same range (about 60–160), all three box plots can be viewed on the calculator screen simultaneously. Remember that the first two plots are heart rates measured in beats per minute while the last plot, recovery time, is measured in seconds.

8. Press [ZOOM]. Select **ZoomStat** to see all three box plots, for resting heart rate. Using the [TRACE] and arrow keys find the median exercise heart rate. The left and right arrows will give you the minimum, maximum, median, and quartiles. The up and down arrows allow you to trace the three plots—Plot 1 is at the top of the screen. You also can see that the maximum the minimum heart rates and recovery times.

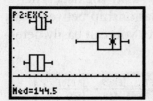 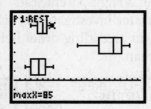 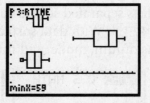

Using the TI-83 Plus Graphing Calculator to Box Plot and Display Statistics

Note: If you have already used the calculator to make histograms, skip to step #3.

1. **Resetting Calculator Memory** Turn on your graphing calculator and press [2nd] [MEM]. Select **Clr All Lists.** Press [ENTER].

2. Name your lists. Press [STAT] and select **Edit.** Scroll up to the title bar (the "top shelf") and over to the first empty list beyond L6 (lists L1–L6 cannot be renamed). The highlighted "A" in the upper corner indicates that you are already in locked-alpha mode. Find and press the desired letters. Press [ENTER] to title your new list for the resting heart rate data. Repeat for the other two variables, exercise heart rate and recovery time. Choose abbreviations that make sense to you—list names are limited to five letters. Then enter all data.

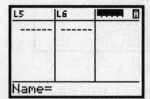

3. Order the data in your lists. Press [2nd] [LIST] and use the right arrow key to select **OPS.** Select the default, **Sort A,** by pressing [ENTER]. The blinking cursor is a signal to insert your list names. Press [2nd] [LIST] and scroll down to select your first list. Then enter a comma. Repeat to select the second and third data lists. Then put a right parentheses ")" after the lists. The commas will keep the lists separated so you can later investigate any relationship between variables if you like. Press [ENTER]. With data sorted (in ascending order here) you can easily determine the minimum, maximum, mode, and median.

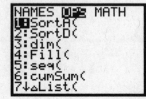 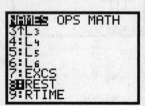 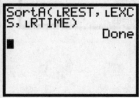 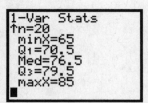

4. For statistical analysis, access the one-variable statistics for each list. Press [STAT] and arrow right to **CALC.** Select the default, **1-Var Stats.** Press [ENTER]. Press [2nd] [LIST] and scroll down to retrieve one of your lists. Press [ENTER] twice. The mean (x) is the first entry, then scroll down to find the minimum (minX), median (Med), and maximum (maxX).

 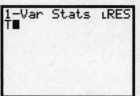 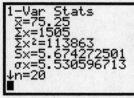

5. Set up your calculator for graphing your data. Press ⌈2nd⌉ [**STAT PLOT**]. Select the default, **Plot 1,** by pressing ⌈ENTER⌉. Use the arrow and ⌈ENTER⌉ keys to turn the plot on and select the fifth graph icon, a standard box plot. For the Xlist, press ⌈2nd⌉ ⌈LIST⌉ and scroll down to find your resting heart rate list. Press ⌈ENTER⌉ twice. Leave Freq at 1.

 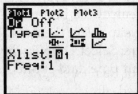 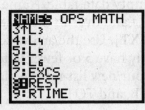 

6. Repeat **Step 5** to set up and turn on Plot 2 and Plot 3. The Xlists will be your exercise heart rate and recovery time lists. Because the data for all three lists is in the same range (about 60–160), all three box plots can be viewed on the calculator screen simultaneously. Remember that the first two plots are heart rates measured in beats per minute while the last plot, recovery time, is measured in seconds.

7. Press ⌈ZOOM⌉ and select **ZoomStat** to see all three box plots for resting heart rate. Using the ⌈TRACE⌉ and arrow keys, find the median exercise heart rate. The left and right arrows will give you the minimum, maximum, median, and quartiles. The up and down arrows allow you to trace the three plots—Plot 1 is at the top of the screen. You can find the maximum and minimum heart rates and recovery times.

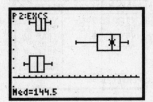 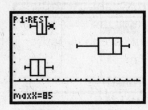 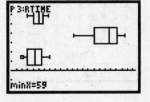

Using the TI-73 Graphing Calculator to Create a Circle Graph

1. **Resetting Calculator Memory** Turn on your graphing calculator and press [2nd] **[MEM]**. Select **ClrAllLists.** Press [ENTER].

2. Press [LIST] to access an empty data table. Name your lists before entering data. Scroll up to the title bar (the "top shelf") and over to the first empty list beyond L6 (lists L1–L6 cannot be renamed). Press [2nd] **[TEXT]**. Use the arrow keys to select the desired letters, pressing [ENTER] after each. Your title can only have 5 or fewer letters. Select **DONE** when you are finished. Press [ENTER] twice to title your new list for the plant type data at Site A. Make three more lists, naming them TOTA, PLNTB, and TOTB.

3. Enter your plant data. Because this data is "categorical" instead of numerical, you must use quotation marks around the first entry only. Place your cursor at the first entry for the list named PLNTA. Press [2nd] **[TEXT]** and scroll first to the quotes and press [ENTER]. Choose your letters, ending with quotes. Notice that a small "c" appears next to the title of a categorical list. Enter the rest of your plant types—you do not need quotes for the rest. Enter the total number of each plant in the next list. Enter data for Site B as well.

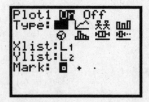  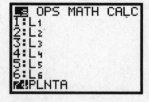 

4. Set up your calculator for graphing your data. Press [2nd] **[PLOT]**. Select **Plot 1** by pressing [ENTER]. Use the arrow keys and [ENTER] to turn the plot on and select the fifth graph icon, a circle graph. For the CategList, press [2nd] **[STAT]** and scroll down to find your list named PLNTA. Press [ENTER] twice. Insert TOTA for Data List. Choose **PERCENT**. Always press [ENTER] to make your choices. Press [GRAPH].

5. Use [TRACE] and the arrow keys to view the labels and numbers for each sector. Notice that the calculator has calculated the percentage for you.

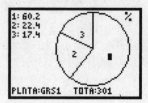

6. Repeat steps 4 and 5 to set up Plot 2 for Site B.

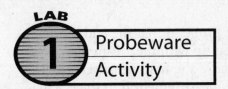

LAB 1 Probeware Activity

How are distance and light intensity related?

As you look up into the night sky, some stars seem to be brighter than others. Do these stars give off different amounts of light or is there another reason that these stars appear to vary in light intensity? In this activity you will explore the relationship between light intensity and distance. You also will investigate why scientists must classify stars according to absolute magnitude and apparent magnitude.

What You'll Investigate

- What is the relationship between light intensity and distance?

Goals

Collect light intensity and distance data.
Investigate the relationship between distance and light intensity.
Discover why stars must be classified according to apparent and absolute magnitude.

Materials

CBL 2 and LabPro unit
TI graphing calculator
Link cable
DataMate program
light-intensity sensor
lamp with 60-watt incandescent bulb
meterstick or measuring tape
masking tape
pen or marker
darkened room

Safety Precautions

- Wear safety goggles and a lab apron during this lab activity.
- Wash your hands before leaving the lab area.

Pre-Lab

1. Does there appear to be a relationship between the intensity of a porch light or street lamp and distance?

2. Based on your experience of light sources and distance, infer the relationship between light intensity and the distance the observer is from the star.

3. Infer why the terms *apparent magnitude* and *absolute* (or *actual*) *magnitude* must be used when referring to the light intensity of stars.

4. What does the graph of the equation $y = 1 / x^2$ look like? If you are not sure, prepare a table using the numbers 1 through 5 for x and graph your results.

SCI 9.e. Construct appropriate graphs from data and develop quantitative statements about the relationships between variables.

Probeware Activity 1 (continued)

Procedure

Part A: Preparing the CBL System

Figure 1

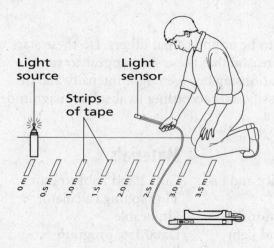

1. Set up the calculator and CBL 2 unit as shown in **Figure 1.** Plug the light intensity probe into channel 1 of the CBL 2 unit.

2. Turn on the calculator and start DataMate. Press CLEAR to reset the program. The light intensity probe should automatically be recognized. If not, turn to page *vi* for instructions on how to manually set up the probe.

3. Select **SETUP.** Press the up arrow key once to select **MODE: TIME GRAPH** and press ENTER.

4. Select **EVENTS WITH ENTRY.** Select **OK** to return to the main screen. Select **START.**

5. You should see a screen that says "PRESS [ENTER] TO COLLECT OR [STO] TO STOP." The light intensity reading will vary as you move the probe. You are ready to collect data.

Part B: Collecting Data

1. Put a strip of masking tape on the lab table or floor starting at the light source. Mark off the distances 1.0, 1.5, 2.0, 2.5, 3.0, and 3.5 meters, moving away from the light source.

2. Position the probe so that the end of the probe is lined up with the 1.0-m line. Press ENTER to record the first measurement. Key the distance measurement into the calculator. Press ENTER.

3. Repeat this procedure for each distance measurement. After you have completed all of your data collection press STO. A graph of the data should appear.

4. Use the arrow keys to scroll through the points on the graph. For each distance (x), write the corresponding light intensity (y) in the **Data Table.** Sketch and label the graph of your experimental data from your calculator screen in the space provided.

5. Press ENTER. Select **QUIT.** Follow the directions on the screen.

Cleanup and Disposal

1. Turn off the graphing calculator and disconnect the light intensity probe and CBL 2.

2. Put the used masking tape into the container designated by your teacher.

3. Return all equipment to the proper location as directed by your teacher.

Experiment Graph: Light Intensity

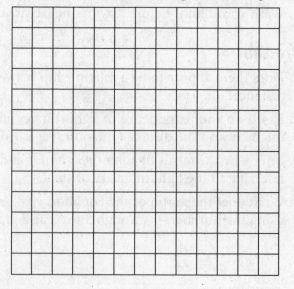

Probeware Activity 1 (continued)

Data Table

Distance (m) (*x*)	Light Intensity (*y*)
1.0	
1.5	
2.0	
2.5	
3.0	
3.5	

Conclude and Apply

1. What is the relationship between light intensity and distance from the light source?

_____

_____

_____

2. What are some of the sources for error in this experiment?

_____

_____

_____

3. Explain why it can be deceptive to use light intensity of stars to estimate their distance from Earth.

_____

_____

_____

_____

4. Compare and contrast your experimental graph with the graph that you drew in pre-lab question number 4.

_____

_____

_____

Notes

LAB 2 Probeware Activity

How fast do you walk?

Whether you walk fast or slow, your speed is almost always changing. When you walk from your classroom to the lunchroom, you may start out walking quickly. If the hall becomes crowded with other students, you probably will slow down. You can describe how fast you walked to the lunchroom by using your average speed for the entire trip or by your instantaneous speed at each point along the way. In this activity, you will use a motion sensor to record your speed as you walk. By analyzing your graph, you can compare your instantaneous speed and average speed.

What You'll Investigate

- How does your instantaneous speed change as you walk?
- How can you use a distance-time graph to determine when your speed is fastest and when it is slowest?

Goals

Measure your change in distance as you walk.
Analyze a distance-time graph.
Estimate instantaneous speed.
Calculate average speed.

Materials

CBL 2 or LabPro unit
TI graphing calculator
link cable
DataMate program
motion sensor
meterstick
masking tape

Safety Precautions

- Wear safety goggles during this lab activity.
- Wash your hands before leaving the lab area.

Pre-Lab

1. Suppose you walk in a straight line away from a table for a distance of 8 meters in 4.3 seconds. You then turn around and walk 8 meters toward the table in 6.8 seconds. What is your average speed as you walk away from the table? Toward the table?
2. Compare the steepness of a line on a distance-time graph when you walk quickly and when you walk slowly.
3. How can you determine where your speed is greatest by looking at a distance-time graph of motion?
4. If you walk away from a motion sensor, stop, turn around, and walk back toward the sensor, what will the distance-time graph of your motion look like for the time you stopped and turned around? Why?

 SCI 1.b. Students know that average speed is the total distance traveled divided by the total time slepsed and that the speed of an object along the path traveled can vary.

Probeware Activity 2 (continued)

Procedure

Part A: Preparing the CBL System

1. Place the motion sensor on the edge of a surface about 1 meter above the floor. Flip up the top of the sensor so that it points along a horizontal, clear space about 2-m long. The motion sensor must have the object that it is measuring in view at all times.

2. Use a meterstick to measure a straight, 2-m path away from the motion sensor. Use masking tape to mark the start and stop lines.

3. Plug the motion sensor connector cable into the DIG/SONIC port on the right side of the CBL 2 unit, as shown in **Figure 1.** Use a link cable to connect the CBL 2 unit to the graphing calculator.

4. Start the DataMate program. Press CLEAR to reset the program.

Figure 1

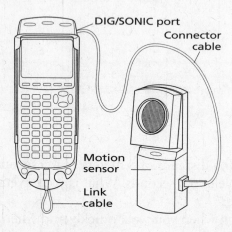

Part B: Collecting Data

1. Stand with your back at least 45 cm from the motion sensor. Have a partner select **START** on the calculator. When you hear the CBL 2 unit make a tone, begin walking along the path away from the motion sensor. Walk to the 2-m mark, turn around, and walk back. The entire trip should last 5 seconds.

2. When the measurement is complete, the calculator will display a screen giving you a choice of graphs. Press ENTER to choose **DIG-DISTANCE,** the distance-time graph.

3. A graph of your motion will appear on the screen. Use the left and right arrow keys to move the cursor along the curve. Data for time (x) and distance (y) will appear at the bottom of the screen. Find the selected time values listed in the **Data Table** on the x-axis of the curve and write the corresponding distance values in the **Data Table.** Round the distance values to the nearest tenth of a meter.

4. Sketch and label the graph on your calculator screen in the space below.

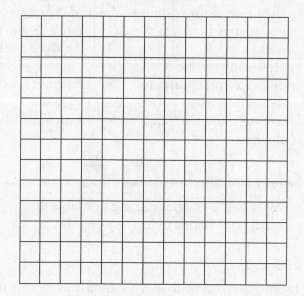

5. When you are finished with the graph, press ENTER. Select **QUIT.** Follow the directions on the calculator screen.

Cleanup and Disposal

1. Turn off the calculator. Disconnect the motion sensor and CBL 2 unit.

2. Return all equipment to the proper location as directed by your teacher. Answer the questions on the following page.

Probeware Activity 2 (continued)

Data Table: Selected Data Points

Distance from Detector (m)	Elapsed Time (s)	Distance Traveled	Change in Time	Instantaneous Speed (m/s)
	0.0	–	–	–
	0.5			
	1.0			
	1.5			
	2.0			
	2.5			
	3.0			
	3.5			
	4.0			
	4.5			
	5.0			

Conclude and Apply

1. Look at the distance-time graph of your data. Without looking at the data table, how can you tell where your speed was fastest and slowest?

   _____

   _____

2. Calculate the distance traveled during each time interval by subtracting the previous distance from the current distance. Calculate the change in time over each time interval by subtracting the previous time from the current time.

3. Calculate the total distance traveled by finding the sum of the values in the *Distance Traveled* column. Divide this value by the total time it took to travel that distance to obtain the average speed.

4. Calculate the approximate instantaneous speed over each time interval. Record the information in the **Data Table.** Round your answers to the nearest tenth. You can obtain an approximate value for your instantaneous speed at each time interval by using this formula:

$$instantaneous\ speed = \frac{distance\ traveled}{change\ in\ time}$$

5. Compare your average speed to your approximate instantaneous speed. Is it possible for average speed to be greater than instantaneous speed? Explain.

   _____

   _____

6. Notice that the instantaneous speed varied as you walked. What would your graph have looked like if you had traveled the entire time at the same instantaneous speed?

Notes

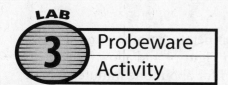

Transforming Energy

LAB 3 Probeware Activity

Everything you do involves a change of energy from one form to another. When you bounce a basketball, potential energy changes to kinetic energy to keep the ball bouncing. Electrical energy is transformed into radiant energy when you flip a light switch.

Friction is a force that converts kinetic energy to thermal energy when two objects rub against one another. Friction converts some of the kinetic energy of a moving match into thermal energy. This thermal energy causes the temperature of the match head to increase until chemicals in the match head catch fire. Friction also changes kinetic energy to thermal energy when the space shuttle returns to Earth. As the shuttle speeds back through the atmosphere, air molecules rush against it. Friction converts kinetic energy from the shuttle into thermal energy. The underside of the shuttle becomes so hot that it must be covered with special heat-resistant tiles to keep from burning up.

In this activity, you will use a temperature probe to look for evidence that friction causes an energy transformation when you shake sand in a jar.

What You'll Investigate

- How can friction cause an energy transformation to occur when you shake a jar of sand?
- What evidence suggests that an energy change has occurred?

Goals

Collect data on energy transformations.

Measure temperature of a solid.

Compare the temperature before and after shaking a solid.

Calculate any temperature changes that occur.

Materials

CBL 2 or LabPro unit
TI graphing calculator
link cable
DataMate program
temperature probe
hot mitt or gloves (2)
sand (250 mL)
clean, plastic jar (approx. 1,000 mL with screw lid)
timer

Safety Precautions

- Wear safety goggles and a lab apron during this lab activity.
- Wash your hands before leaving the lab area.
- Extinguish all flames before beginning this activity.

Pre-Lab

1. What is kinetic energy?

2. Describe how friction produces an energy transformation that makes your hands feel warm when you rub them together rapidly.

3. Hypothesize what energy transformation will occur when you shake sand in a jar. How is friction between the sand particles related to this?

4. Why is it important to wear gloves while holding the jar during shaking and temperature readings?

SCI 2.d. Students know how to identify separately the two or more forces that are acting on a single static object, including gravity, elastic forces due to tension or compression in matter, and friction.

Probeware Activity 3 (continued)

Procedure

Part A: Preparing the CBL System

1. Set up the calculator and CBL 2 unit, as shown in **Figure 1**. Plug the temperature probe into channel 1 of the CBL 2 unit.

2. Turn on the calculator and start DataMate. Press CLEAR to reset the program. The temperature probe should be recognized automatically. If not, turn to page *vi* for instructions on how to set up the probe manually.

Figure 1

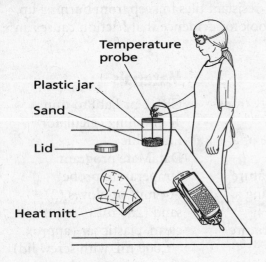

Temperature probe

Plastic jar

Sand

Lid

Heat mitt

Part B: Collecting Data

1. Fill the plastic jar about $^1/_4$ full of sand.

2. The calculator screen should display the room air temperature measured by the probe in the upper right corner of the screen. Record the room air temperature, to one decimal place, in the **Data Table.**

3. Place the temperature probe into the sand, as shown in **Figure 1** and allow it to sit undisturbed for about one minute. Record the temperature, to one decimal place, in the **Data Table,** as the start temperature.

4. For the next six minutes you will alternate shaking the closed jar of sand for one minute and then measuring the sand temperature during the next minute. Tighten the lid securely on the jar. Put on a pair of gloves and pick up the jar. Always hold the jar with two gloved hands. Shake the jar vigorously (hard) for one minute.

5. Remove the jar's lid and place the temperature probe into the sand. After about 30 to 45 seconds, record the sand's temperature in the **Data Table.** Tighten the lid back on the jar and repeat the procedure three times. Record the temperature for each trial in the **Data Table.**

6. Select **QUIT.** Follow the directions on the calculator screen.

Cleanup and Disposal

1. Turn off the graphing calculator and disconnect the temperature probe and the CBL 2 unit.

2. Clean off the temperature probe with a paper towel.

3. Return the CBL 2 and other laboratory equipment to its proper place as directed by your teacher.

Probeware Activity 3 (continued)

Data Table: Sand Temperature

Time (minutes)	Task	Temperature °C
Start	Measure temperature	
0 – 1	Shake jar	
1 – 2	Measure temperature	
2 – 3	Shake jar	
3 – 4	Measure temperature	
4 – 5	Shake jar	
5 – 6 (End)	Measure temperature	

Conclude and Apply

1. Compare the sand temperature readings. Describe any change.

_____

_____

2. Suggest a possible explanation for your observations.

_____

_____

3. As you shook the jar of sand, chemical energy from the food you ate changed to kinetic energy in your muscles. This, in turn, provided kinetic energy to the sand. In the space below, create a concept map showing the series of energy transformations from the food you ate to the thermal energy released to the air.

4. How do you think your results would change if you shook the sand faster? How would the results change if you shook the sand longer? Explain.

_____

_____

_____

5. A meteor is a meteoroid that falls through Earth's atmosphere. Based on the results you obtained in this experiment, explain why a meteor appears as a streak of light in the night sky.

_____

_____

Notes

Endothermic and Exothermic Processes

When a substance dissolves in water, a change in energy usually occurs. Although a change in energy can be a sign of a chemical change, the dissolving of a substance is a physical change. The water molecules break apart into positive and negative parts and surround the particles of the substance that is dissolving. In some cases, dissolving releases heat energy into the surroundings. Processes that release heat energy are called *exothermic.* In other cases, dissolving absorbs heat energy from the surroundings. Processes that absorb heat are called *endothermic.* How can you tell if heat energy is released or absorbed? In this activity you will collect data and search for clues to determine which type of heat energy transfer is taking place.

What You'll Investigate

- What happens when $CaCl_2$ and KCl are added to water?
- Will these processes produce temperature changes?

Goals

Measure the change in temperature when substances are added to water.
Calculate any change in water temperature that occurs during the process.
Graph temperature changes over time.

Materials

CBL 2 or LabPro unit
TI graphing calculator
link cable
DataMate program
temperature probe
400-mL beaker
100-mL beaker
plastic spoon
glass stirring rod
distilled water
    (room temperature)
5.0g calcium chloride ($CaCl_2$)
5.0g potassium chloride (KCl)

Safety Precautions

- Wear safety goggles and a lab apron during this lab activity.
- Report any spills to your teacher.
- Do not taste, eat, or drink any materials used in the lab.
- Wash your hands before leaving the lab area.

Pre-Lab

1. What is a physical change?

2. What are examples of physical change?

3. What is an exothermic process?

4. What is an endothermic process?

 SCI 5.c. Students know chemical reactions usually liberate heat or absorb heat.

Probeware Activity 4 (continued)

Procedure

Part A: Preparing the CBL System

1. Set up the calculator and CBL 2 unit, as shown in **Figure 1**. Plug the temperature probe into channel 1 of the CBL 2 unit.

2. Turn on the calculator and start DataMate. Press to reset the program. The temperature probe should be recognized automatically. If not, turn to page *vi* for instructions on how to set up the probe manually.

Figure 1

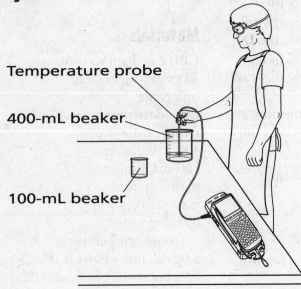

Temperature probe

400-mL beaker

100-mL beaker

Part B: Collecting Data

1. Add 100 mL of room-temperature water to the 400-mL beaker.

2. Place the temperature probe in the water.

3. Use a balance to measure 5.0 g of potassium chloride on a piece of weighing paper or in a weighing dish.

4. On the graphing calculator, select **START** to begin the data collection. About five seconds after data collection has begun, carefully add the potassium chloride to the water. Make sure all of the potassium chloride is emptied into the water. Data will be collected for 180 seconds.

5. Using a glass stirring rod, gently stir the water in the beaker for about 20 seconds to help the potassium chloride dissolve.

6. After 180 seconds have lapsed, the calculator will display a graph of temperature versus time with temperature on the *y*-axis and time on the *x*-axis. Sketch and label this graph in your **Science Journal.**

Part C: Examining the Data

1. Return to the main screen by pressing ENTER.

2. Select **ANALYZE.**

3. Select **STATISTICS.**

4. Press ENTER to select the beginning of the temperature graph. Use the right arrow key to select the last temperature data point reached. Press ENTER to select this point.

5. Your calculator will display the minimum and maximum temperatures reached. Determine which of these is the starting temperature and which is the ending temperature—the temperature after all of the solid dissolved. Record these temperatures in the **Data Table.** When you are finished, press ENTER. Select **RETURN TO MAIN SCREEN.**

6. Rinse your beaker thoroughly and repeat parts **B** and **C** using 5 g of calcium chloride.

7. When you are finished, press ENTER. Select **RETURN TO MAIN SCREEN.** Select **QUIT.** Follow the directions on the screen.

Cleanup and Disposal

1. Turn off the graphing calculator and disconnect the temperature probe and CBL 2 unit.

2. Clean and return all equipment as directed by your teacher and answer the questions on the following page.

Probeware Activity 4 (continued)

Data Table: Dissolving of KCl and CaCl$_2$

Substance	Starting Temperature (°C)	Ending Temperature (°C)	Temperature Change (°C)	Type of Process
Potassium chloride (KCl)				
Calcium chloride (CaCl$_2$)				

Conclude and Apply

1. Calculate the temperature change for each substance by subtracting the starting temperature from the ending temperature. Record your results in the **Data Table.** How are these temperature changes different?

_____

_____

_____

2. Which process is endothermic and which is exothermic?

_____

_____

3. Look at your graphs. Suggest a possible explanation for why the temperature of the water changed rapidly at first and then leveled off.

_____

_____

_____

4. From your results, infer what the result might be if twice as much potassium chloride was added to the same amount of water.

_____

_____

_____

Notes

LAB 5 Probeware Activity

Let the races begin!

Sledding down a hill in the snow, coasting down a hill on your bike, or speeding down a hill in a roller coaster would not be the same without a steep hill. You know that the higher the hill, the faster you'll be going when you reach the bottom. This is because objects at the top of a hill have potential energy. The amount of potential energy that an object has depends upon its height above Earth. This potential energy is converted into kinetic energy—energy of motion, when the object falls downward. Whether the hill is steep or has a gentle slope, your speed at the bottom depends on the height of the hill. In this experiment you will collect distance, velocity, and acceleration data by rolling a toy car down a board at two different heights.

What You'll Investigate

- How does the height of a ramp affect speed and acceleration?

Goals

Collect distance, velocity, and acceleration data.
Compare the graphs for each trial.
Identify sources of experimental error.

Materials

CBL 2 or LabPro unit
TI graphing calculator
link cable
DataMate program
motion sensor
board (at least 1.5 m long)
toy car or lab cart

Safety Precautions 🥽 🧤 ✋

- Wear safety goggles and a lab apron during this lab activity.
- Wash your hands before leaving the lab area.

Pre-Lab

1. How are distance, speed, time, and acceleration related?

2. How does the kinetic and potential energy of an object change as the object falls?

3. The motion sensor works in a way that is similar to the way a radar-speed detector works. In looking at the motion sensor, the toy car, and the board, what things must be taken into consideration before starting your investigation?

4. Where are the sources of friction in this lab?

 SCI 1.f. Students know how to interpret graphs of position versus time and graphs of speed versus time for motion in a single direction.

Probeware Activity 5 (continued)

Procedure

Part A: Preparing the CBL System

Figure 1

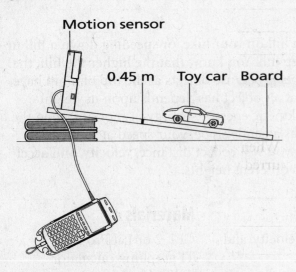

Motion sensor

0.45 m   Toy car   Board

1. Set up the calculator and CBL 2 unit, as shown in **Figure 1.** The motion sensor should be plugged into the DIG/SONIC channel that is located on the right-hand side of the CBL 2 unit.

2. Turn on the calculator and start DataMate. Press (CLEAR) to reset the program.

Part B: Collecting Data

1. Use textbooks to elevate the board, as shown in **Figure 1.** Put just enough textbooks under the board so that the car rolls down the ramp.

2. Position the motion sensor at the top of the ramp so that it can "see" the car as it travels down the ramp. The car must be placed at least 45 cm from the motion sensor for the sensor to operate properly. When the car and motion sensor are in place, you will hear a series of soft clicks from the motion detector.

3. Select **START** on the calculator and release the car.

Part C: Examining the Data

1. After the run is complete, the screen will display a choice of three graphs: DIG-DISTANCE, DIG-VELOCITY, AND DIG-ACCELERATION. Select **DIG-VELOCITY** to display a velocity-time graph.

2. Sketch and label this graph in your **Science Journal.**

3. Use the arrow keys to obtain the maximum *y*-value (velocity) and the *x*-value (time) that maximum velocity occurred. Write these data in the **Data Table.** Press (ENTER).

4. Select **DIG-ACCELERATION** to display an acceleration-time graph.

5. Sketch and label this graph in your **Science Journal.**

6. Use the arrow keys to obtain the maximum acceleration and the time that the maximum acceleration occurred. Write these data in the **Data Table.** Press (ENTER).

7. Select **DIG-DISTANCE** to display a distance-time graph.

8. Sketch and label this graph in your **Science Journal.**

9. Press (ENTER). Select **MAIN SCREEN.**

10. Repeat part B and part C, Steps 1–9, using additional textbooks to elevate the ramp at a steeper angle. Record the data for each trial in the **Data Table.** Sketch and label each graph.

11. From the main screen, select **QUIT.** Follow the directions on the screen.

Cleanup and Disposal

1. Turn off the graphing calculator and disconnect the motion sensor and CBL 2 unit.

2. Return all equipment to the proper location as directed by your teacher and answer the following questions.

Probeware Activity 5 (continued)

Data Table: Run Data

	First Run	Second Run
Maximum velocity		
Time maximum velocity occurred		
Maximum acceleration		
Time maximum acceleration occurred		

Conclude and Apply

1. When did the velocity of the car reach a maximum? When did the acceleration of the car reach a maximum? Explain possible reasons why these occurred when they did.

_____

_____

_____

_____

2. Using your graphs, determine when the car appears to have completed the run or moved out of sight of the motion sensor.

_____

_____

3. If friction were not present, what would the graphs for velocity and acceleration look like?

_____

_____

4. Identify possible sources of experimental error in your experiment.

_____

_____

5. How did increasing the height of the car's starting position affect the potential energy of the car?

_____

6. Explain why increasing the height of the car's starting position increased the car's speed at the bottom of the board.

_____

_____

Notes